Mr. Wizard's

SCIENCE

SECRETS

By Don Herbert

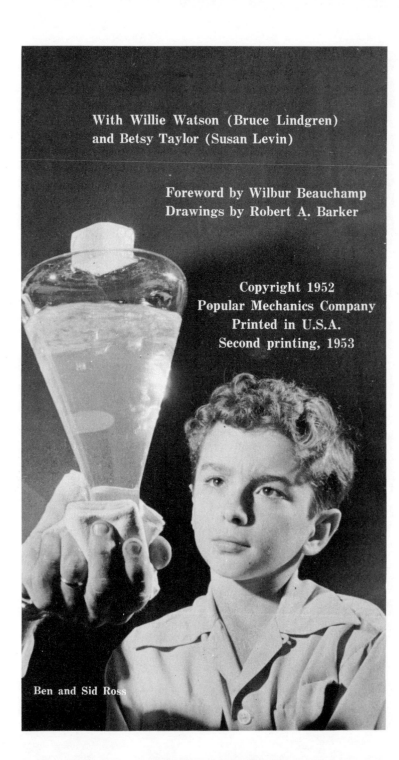

With Willie Watson (Bruce Lindgren)
and Betsy Taylor (Susan Levin)

Foreword by Wilbur Beauchamp
Drawings by Robert A. Barker

Ben and Sid Ross

WHEN YOU BUY A BOOK *such as this you expect to have some fun doing the things it suggests. Many times, however, you are fooled. When you actually try to do the experiments you find that you don't have or can't get the needed materials and equipment. Or you find that the directions are so poorly written that you cannot follow them. You may even find the experiments won't work.*

Here is a book, however, that will give you your money's worth. If you want to do some interesting experiments with materials you usually can find at home and with apparatus you can make easily, this is the book for you. You will be amazed, and so will your friends, with the "magical" tricks you can do. Of course, science is not magic. There are certain laws which nature follows. The experiments will help you understand these laws and then to explain the "magical" tricks.

Mr. Wizard has done more for you than to tell you how to do the experiments. He also has explained why the experiment works. If you are interested in science, this is the most valuable part of the book. It is easy to build a model airplane or glider, but the most interesting thing about an airplane is, "What keeps it in the air?"

You can find the answer to this and many other questions in this book. Mr. Wizard's explanations are ones you really can understand. When your friends ask you questions about the experiments you perform, you'll be ready with the answers.

It's a good book.

Wilbur L. Beauchamp
Professor of Education,
The University of Chicago

Chapters

Photos not otherwise credited
were taken by Frank P. Fritz
of the Popular Mechanics staff

THIS IS A BOOK OF SCIENCE SECRETS. *But there's more to science than the secrets in this book. Science begins with the parts of an atom, ends with the whole universe and includes everything in between.*

But a part of science deals with the world you can see, hear and feel all around you. That's the part of science that's fun to investigate for yourself right at home. Milk bottles are your flasks, glasses your beakers and the whole house your laboratory.

Just knowing the secret isn't enough, however. You've got to understand, try and perfect an experiment before it will work smoothly. When it doesn't work, figure out why it doesn't and do it again.

If you don't happen to have the exact materials the experiment calls for, maybe you can do it another way with materials you do have. No matter what you use to do it with, doing the experiment is the best fun . . . and the best way to know the science secret.

Don Herbert

MR. WIZARD

DEDICATED *to M.D.H. and H.A.R.D.*
and
To the scientists who showed me why . . .
To all the teachers who showed me how . . .
And to all of you who want to try.

Chapter One

Right in front of your nose

DO YOU LIKE MYSTERIES AND MAGIC? If you do, why not investigate the mysteries and the magic in the world around you? That's what Willy Watson and sometimes Betsy Taylor and I do every week. They're kids who live in my neighborhood and come over to my home laboratory just to solve the mysteries of the things they see and do every day. They're usually amazed at what they discover and I think you will be too because there's more mystery and magic than you ever thought of right in front of your nose.

Take a good look at the space right in front of your nose. Now you may not be able to see anything but right there in front of your nose is one of the most important things in the world to you. I mean air!

Of course, you know there's air in front of your nose but you didn't think about it, did you? That's because you're used to it. You walk around in it and breathe it . . . and never think about it. Let's take a good look at the air. I think you'll be surprised.

Did you know that at this very moment you're sitting at the bottom of an ocean? The air we live in is very much like an ocean. In fact, air is so much like water you can even pour it. Here's all you have to do:

EXPERIMENT 1

Materials: Two drinking glasses (same size)

Large basin, pail or the kitchen sink (container must be deep enough for glasses to be under water when standing upright)

Fill the container with water and place glass A under water so it fills with water.

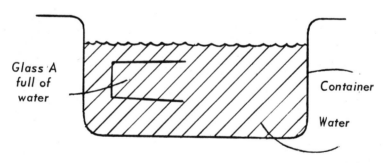

Glass A full of water

Container

Water

Hold glass A by the bottom and raise it out of the water, keeping the mouth of the glass under water. It will remain full of water. Turn glass B upside down and put it straight down into water. Notice water does not run into glass because it's full of air.

Now tip the glass of air (B) under the glass of water (A) and see the air bubble up into the glass

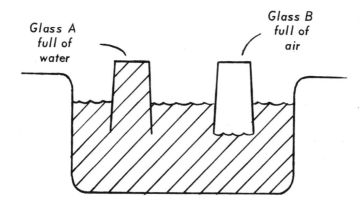

Glass A full of water

Glass B full of air

of water forcing the water out. As you pour air out of glass B, water will pour into it.

Glass A which was full of air is now full of water and glass B which was full of water is now full of air. You can pour the air back and forth from glass to glass!

You see, you pour air upside down from the way you pour water. The water makes the air visible to you in the form of bubbles and makes the bubbles go up.

Did you notice that you could see the air taking up space in the glass under water? Well, the air fills up the space around us and actually weighs some-

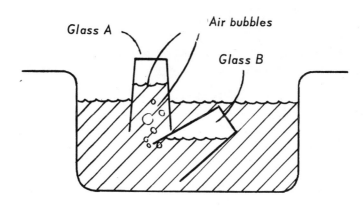

Glass A

Air bubbles

Glass B

Glass A was *full* of water, now *full* of air

Glass B was *full of air*, now *full of water*

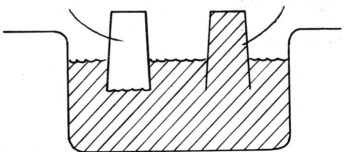

thing, just like water does. Hold out your hand, palm up. Right on top of your hand is a tall column of air that goes up further than you can see. Can you feel the weight of it? Of course, you can't! Yet, if the air weighs something why can't you feel it? Let's solve that mystery right now.

EXPERIMENT 2

Materials: Drinking glass

Piece of cardboard or waxed paper a little larger than the glass is round

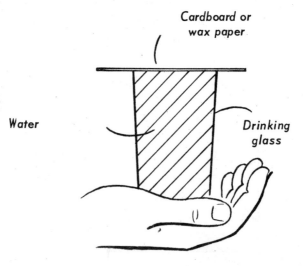

Cardboard or wax paper

Water

Drinking glass

Fill the glass with water to the brim and place cardboard or waxed paper on top. What's holding the cardboard up? The glass, of course.

Now set the glass on the palm of your right hand and place the palm of your left hand on top of the cardboard. Quickly turn the glass upside down, being careful to keep the cardboard in place. Now what's holding the cardboard up? Your hand, of course.

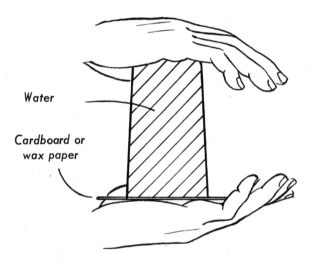

Water

Cardboard or wax paper

With your right hand holding the glass firmly, slowly take your left hand out from under the cardboard. Now what's holding the cardboard up? This is how Betsy looked when she tried it using waxed paper.

Better try this over a sink because you're go-

ing to make the cardboard and the water fall in a minute.

The fact that the cardboard doesn't fall and holds the water in the glass looks like magic, doesn't it? Well, it isn't. It's just another example of the things that go on all around us that look like magic. Now here's the secret of why the card doesn't fall:

Remember I said that the air is like an ocean and we're living in the bottom of it? Well, the air is pushing against the glass in all directions indicated by the little arrows.

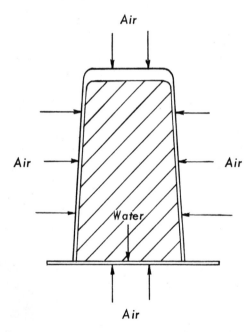

Notice the air pushes down on the top, in from the sides and from underneath up. If the glass were in an ocean, the water would push in all around the same way. Now, while it's true that the air is pushing in all around, the glass is rigid and keeps the air from pushing against the water in the glass. Down at the bottom where the cardboard is, the air pushes up on the cardboard and it pushes up against the water. Now you expect the water to fall because you know the force of gravity is pulling it down. But the air is pushing up harder than gravity is pulling down and, because the card is held tight against the glass so no air can get in and push down on top of the water, the cardboard is "glued" to the glass and the water doesn't fall. What do you think will happen if you let a little air in? Try it and see. Put your finger at the edge of the cardboard and push down until a couple of bubbles of air get in and can help push down on top of the water. The cardboard and the water in the glass will fall down just as you expected them to.

Now do you see why you can't feel the weight of the air pushing down on your hand? You can understand how the air pushing down exerts pressure, and you just saw how the air pushes up . . . that's what held the card up to the glass. Actually, the air is pushing in from all directions . . . even from the *inside* of your hand *out*. Do you notice the shoes that you're wearing? Probably not, because you're so used to them, and that's exactly why you can't feel the pressure of the air. You're so used to it. You were born and live in this "atmospheric pressure."

Now see if you can solve this mystery:

EXPERIMENT 3

Materials: **Milk bottle**

Enough cheesecloth to cover the mouth of the bottle with two layers

A pitcher of water

Rubber band or string

13

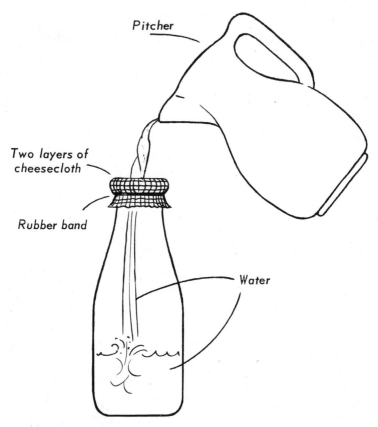

Pitcher

Two layers of cheesecloth

Rubber band

Water

Fasten a *double* layer of cheesecloth over the mouth of the milk bottle with the rubber band or string. When you fill the milk bottle with water from the pitcher it goes into the milk bottle very easily because the cheesecloth is so thin.

Now set the pitcher down on the table and quickly turn the milk bottle full of water upside down over it. The water went through the cheesecloth into the bottle all right. Why won't it come *out* through the cheesecloth now?

It looks like the water ought to run out of the milk bottle without any trouble because the cheese-

14

cloth is so full of holes. But the cheesecloth . . . and air . . . are the keys to the solution of the mystery. You see, the cheesecloth spreads the water over the mouth of the milk bottle, preventing the air from getting in and pushing down on top of the water. But the air is still pushing up just like it did when it held up the cardboard to the glass of water in Experiment 2. Tip the bottle a little bit and you'll see the air flow in on the top side while the water flows out on the bottom side of the mouth of the bottle. The gurgling sound is the result of the air and water bumping into each other as they pass.

Fran Byrne

You probably didn't think about it but you allow for this every time you pour anything from a bottle. You tip the bottle just enough to let the liquid run out of the bottom and the air to run in the top of the mouth.

Remember when you held your hand out I said there was a tall column of air above it going away up into the sky but that you can't feel it because it pushes in all directions and you're used to it? Scientists have special ways of weighing the air and they found out that it weighs quite a bit. You've seen postage stamps that are about this big?

Well, the air on that little bit of surface weighs 14.7 pounds. Scientists call it air pressure and say that air pressure is 14.7 pounds per square inch. To give you some idea of how much weight that actually is, imagine you're carrying 15 pounds of butter.

Now the air pressure is less on the top of a mountain than it is at the level of the sea because the column of air from the top of the mountain to the top of the ocean of air above it is not so deep and, therefore, doesn't weigh as much. And the air pressure at the bottom of a mine is more than it is at the level of the sea because the column of air from the bottom of the mine up to the top of the ocean of air above it is deeper. But at the level of the sea the air pressure is 14.7 pounds. Scientists call it normal atmospheric pressure. Can you imagine how it would feel to hold out your hand and have about 15 pounds of sugar on every little space the size of a postage stamp! You couldn't possibly hold your hand up. And imagine what it would be like to try and stand up and walk around with all that weight pushing down on every square inch of your head and shoulders! You couldn't even stand up, let alone walk! It's a good thing the air pushes in all directions, including pushing out from inside of you.

When you know how to do it you can make the tremendous pressure of the air help you break a stick right in two. Here's how you do it:

EXPERIMENT 4

Materials: **Two sheets of newspaper without holes or tears**

Slats from a wooden apple or orange crate

Stout stick or baseball bat

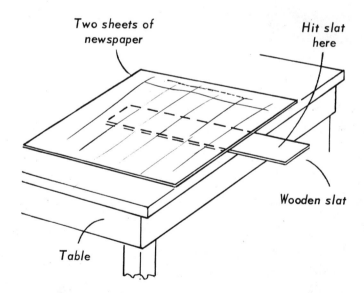

Two sheets of
newspaper

Hit slat
here

Wooden slat

Table

Lay the wooden slat on a table and cover it with the two sheets of newspaper.

First smooth out the paper carefully all over the table and then with the baseball bat come down

hard on the piece of wooden slat sticking out from the edge of the table. Instead of the paper and slat flying off the table as Willy expected when he tried it, he broke the slat in two right at the edge of the table!

Here's the secret of how the air pressure helped break that slat in two. You know by now that the air is pushing down on top of the newspaper. Even though the slat is lying on the table there is still air pushing up between it and the table. If you push down slowly on the slat instead of hitting it with the bat, the other end of it and the newspaper will go up because the air has a chance to flow in under the newspaper and push up under the slat. But when you come down hard with the baseball bat, the other end starts to go up fast! That little bit of air underneath expands until it's very, very thin . . . almost nothing, in fact. It can't push very hard compared to the air on top of the paper pushing down. None of the air on the outside can get in to help that thin air push up because the newspaper prevents the air from getting in for a fraction of a second. So the weight of the whole column of air above the newspaper holds that end of the slat down tight with about the same force as though there were five tons of coal piled up there! With all that pressure on one end of the slat and you hitting the other end with a baseball bat, there's no mystery about why it breaks in two!

So far we've talked about ordinary atmospheric pressure. But what happens when we somehow increase the pressure of the air? All sorts of interesting things. For instance:

EXPERIMENT 5

Materials: **A smooth tube of glass or metal about 6 inches long**

A wooden plunger that fits inside the tube loosely

Slices of potato about ¾ of an inch thick

Push the tube through a potato slice and cut out a piece of potato in much the same way that you cut out cookies with a cookie cutter. This will seal up the end of the tube. Now do the same thing with the other end.

Slowly push one of the potato plugs further into the tube with the wooden plunger. Then, aiming the other end at a suitable target, push the plunger hard and fast. There will be a loud pop and the piece

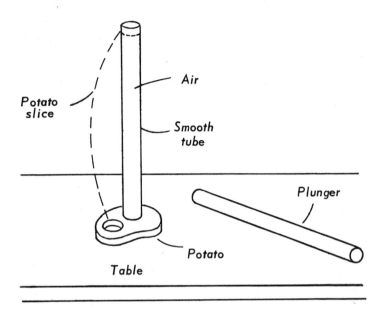

of potato at the front end will travel like a bullet.

Simply push the remaining piece of potato to the front end, cut a new piece of potato with the tube and you are ready to "fire" again.

Notice you don't actually touch the front potato with the plunger. The potato at each end seals the air inside the tube and when you push the plunger you put the air inside the tube under greater pressure than the atmospheric pressure around it. As you push the plunger the increased pressure inside the tube builds up until it is strong enough to over-

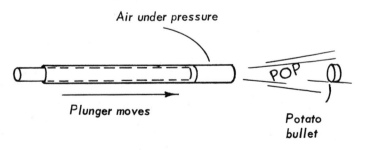

come the friction holding the front potato in the tube and suddenly, when the pressure becomes great enough, it pushes the potato out with considerable force. The loud bang is caused by the sudden release of the air under pressure in the tube.

When you use BB's instead of a piece of a potato, have a better compressing chamber for the air, can pump several times to build up more pressure and can release that pressure with a trigger—you're using an air rifle. When you put a special hammer head on the front end and build and release strong pressure automatically, you've got an air hammer, used to drill holes, drive spikes and rivets and break up pavements.

Using compressed air (air under compression or pressure) you can make a water fountain.

EXPERIMENT 6

Materials: **Soda bottle**

One-hole rubber stopper

Piece of glass tubing slightly shorter than the length of the bottle

Short piece of glass tubing formed into a nozzle

Short piece of rubber tubing to fit glass tubing

Fill bottle about half full of water and place the stopper and tubing into position.

Blow hard into the nozzle. Bubbles of air will come out of the bottom of the glass tubing because you are blowing air into the tubing. When you have blown as hard as you can, move back quickly, because water will shoot out of the nozzle. How high it goes depends on how hard you can blow.

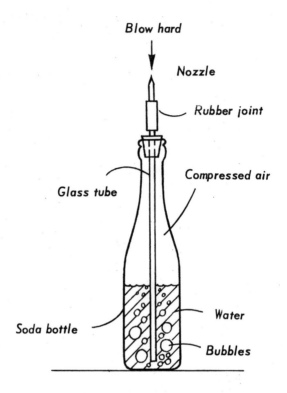

You should have no trouble explaining why the water shoots out. When you blew hard into the tube you forced air down through the tube and air bubbles rose to the top of the water and were added to the air already there. The harder you blew the more air was forced into the bottle and the more the air was compressed above the water. When you stopped blowing, the pressure of the air pushed on the water and moved it up the tube with enough force to make a fountain.

You can make a more powerful stream of water come from a nozzle by putting more air pressure on the water. Instead of blowing to make the pressure try this:

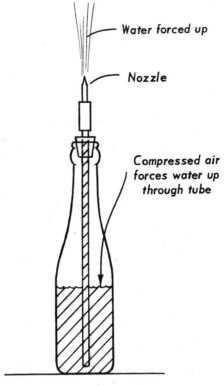

Water forced up

Nozzle

Compressed air
forces water up
through tube

EXPERIMENT 7

Materials: Soda bottle

One-hole stopper for bottle

One-hole stopper to fit water faucet

Short length of glass tubing

Short length of glass tubing fashioned into
a nozzle

Piece of rubber hose

Wire or string to make joints secure

Water in the pipe lines in the house is under
pressure and you release that pressure when you
open the faucet. By holding the stopper tightly

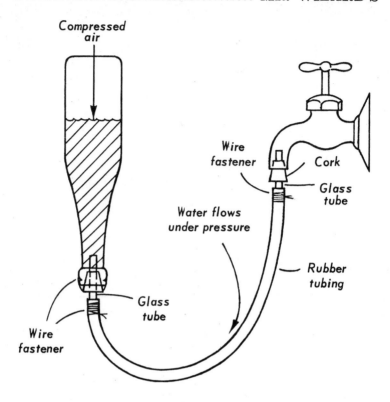

against the mouth of the faucet, the water pressure in the pipes forces water into the bottle and compresses the air. Pinch the tube to hold the pressure and turn off the faucet. Aim the nozzle at an appropriate target and let go of the tubing. The air under pressure above the water in the bottle will push the water out with great force.

Better try this outside because you'll need a long range and walls and furniture aren't supposed to get wet.

EXPERIMENT 8

Materials: Soda bottle

Rubber toy balloon

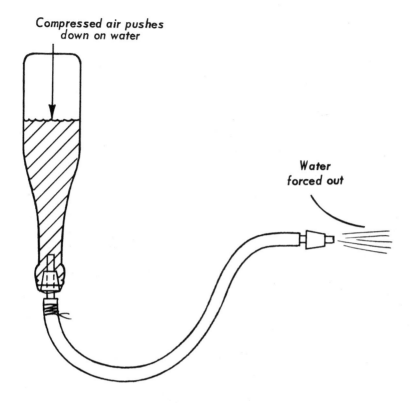

Compressed air pushes
down on water

Water
forced out

Ever blow up a balloon inside a bottle? It's a lot harder than you think because you'll have to blow up the bottle too!

With a pencil push the balloon into the neck of the soda bottle, fold back the mouth of the balloon and stretch it over the mouth of the bottle.

Now blow up the balloon . . . if you can. You'll find you can't blow the balloon up very much because as you begin to put air into the balloon the pressure expands it just as you'd expect. But as the balloon expands it begins to crowd the air trapped in the bottle. As you compress that air it pushes back harder and harder until it's pushing back as hard as you can blow.

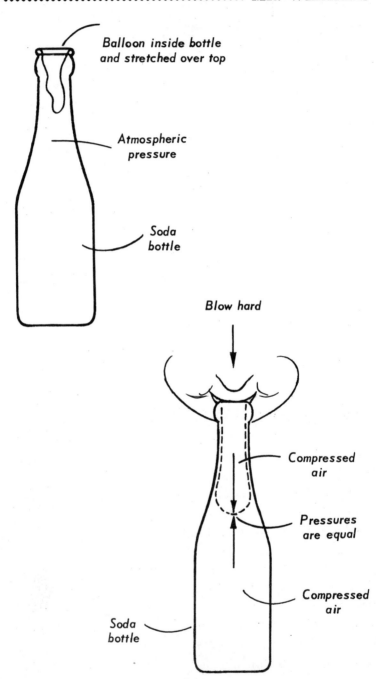

Balloon inside bottle
and stretched over top

Atmospheric
pressure

Soda
bottle

Blow hard

Compressed
air

Pressures
are equal

Compressed
air

Soda
bottle

To make the balloon bigger you'd have to blow hard enough to make the bottle bigger too. Try this on your friends but not before you have done the experiments in the next chapter because then you'll be able to show them how to blow up the balloon inside the bottle without really blowing at all!

While you've got the balloon handy, though, you can ask your friends to do this:

EXPERIMENT 9

Materials: A balloon

Two cups

Here's the puzzle I asked Willy: How can you pick up two cups with a balloon without using the handles of the cups?

Arrange the cups and the balloon as I did, and blow up the balloon. As you blow, the pressure of the air forces the sides of the balloon into the cups.

Fran Byrne

Still more pressure pushes the sides of the balloon against the inside of the cups hard enough so they won't slip when you pick up the ballon by the neck (better use old cups as I did . . . just in case).

So whether the air is under ordinary atmospheric pressure or still greater pressure, it's full of mysteries . . . until you solve them. Did you realize that sometimes there's a sort of hole in the air? Let's investigate the amazing hole in the air scientists call a "vacuum."

Chapter Two

Holes in the air

EVEN THOUGH YOUR FRIENDS won't be able to blow up a balloon inside of a bottle you can do it without blowing at all—if you make a "hole" in the air in the bottle.

EXPERIMENT 10

Materials: Milk bottle

> **Piece of paper folded so you can slip it into the bottle easily**
>
> **Matches**
>
> **Balloon**

There is no need to tell you there's air around the bottle and inside of it under normal atmospheric pressure. To make a hole in the air inside the bottle all you have to do is change some of it into something else that takes up less space. That's exactly what

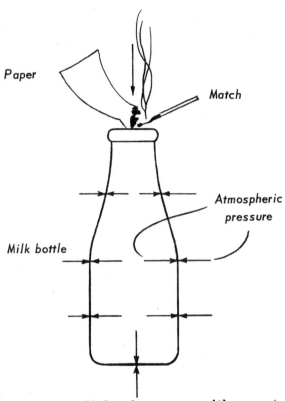

Paper

Match

Atmospheric pressure

Milk bottle

you do when you light the paper with a match and slip it inside the bottle.

As the paper burns, the heat produced expands the air and some of it escapes from the bottle. When the air cools, it contracts; the atmospheric pressure is greater, and the balloon is forced into the bottle.

Note that some of the arrows that indicate air pressure are missing inside the bottle because part of the air is changed. What's left takes up less space and can't push as hard. We now have a "hole" or partial vacuum inside the bottle. The air outside the bottle, pushing in from all directions, will try to fill up that vacuum. It's very much like when you put your hand down into a pail full of sand and take a

handful from the middle of it. As you pull the handful of sand out the rest of the sand flows in to fill
up the hole you made. The same sort of thing happens in the air. However, the sides of the bottle are
hard and hold back the air so that it can't flow in
and fill up the "hole." But the balloon on top of the
mouth of the bottle will stretch. The atmospheric
pressure pushes down and blows up the balloon inside the bottle until the air beneath the balloon can
push back with the same force as atmospheric pressure.

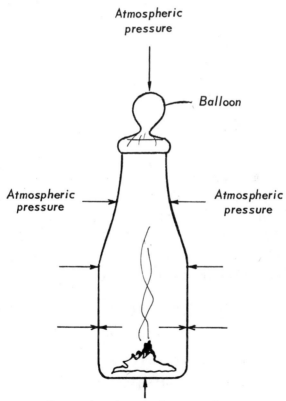

Burning paper combines with some
of air creating "hole" or vacuum

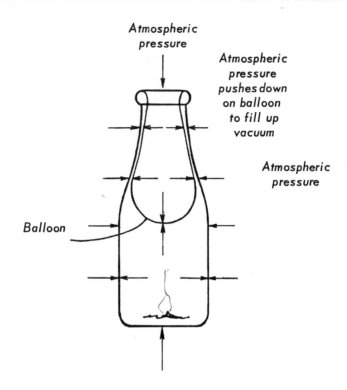

Atmospheric
pressure

Atmospheric
pressure
pushes down
on balloon
to fill up
vacuum

Atmospheric
pressure

Balloon

Now you've blown up a balloon inside a bottle without actually blowing at all.

When you try to get the balloon out of the bottle you'll have to put a pencil or tube down the neck of the bottle between the balloon and the glass.

Another trick you can do with a vacuum is "glue" two glasses together.

EXPERIMENT 11

Materials: Two drinking glasses of the same size

Piece of paper and match

A blotter collar made to fit the rim of the glasses

Scissors

The blotter used for the collar must be absorbent on both sides. Out of the blotter cut a circle with a diameter half an inch larger than the rim of the drinking glasses. Then cut a large round hole in the center of the circle to form a collar. Wet the collar thoroughly and place it on top of one of the glasses on the table. Light the paper with a match and hold the second glass upside down near the first glass.

Quickly toss the burning paper in the glass on the table and just as quickly place the second glass on the first so their rims are one above the other with the blotter collar in between. When the burning paper goes out, you can raise both the glasses off the table by picking up the top one. The wet blotter collar acts as a seal to keep out the air and the glasses

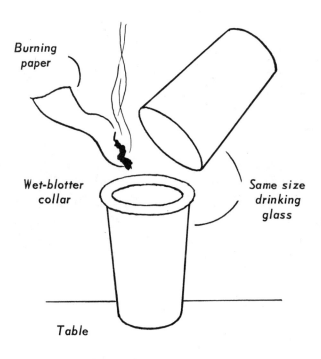

Burning paper

Wet-blotter collar

Same size drinking glass

Table

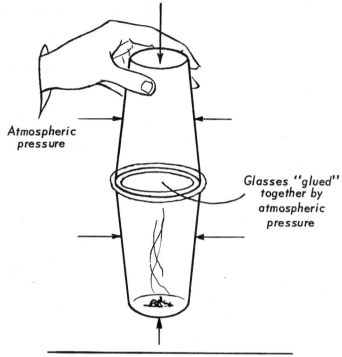

Atmospheric
pressure

Glasses "glued"
together by
atmospheric
pressure

Table

are "glued" together by the atmospheric pressure trying to get in and fill up the partial vacuum inside.

Before people realized that there was such a thing as atmospheric pressure they noticed that whenever there was a "hole" in the air, the vacuum seemed to suck something into it. They called it "suction." And that's why you call the little rubber gadget that sticks to smooth surfaces a "suction cup." It should be called an atmospheric-pressure cup or a vacuum cup because it has no sucking power at all. It works like this:

EXPERIMENT 12

Materials: A "suction" cup

Mineral oil

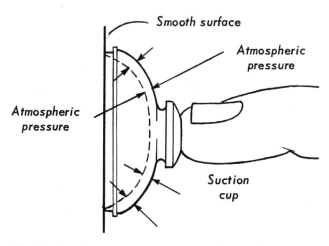

Hold the "suction" cup lightly against a smooth surface such as a window, bathtub or tile wall. There's atmospheric pressure inside and out.

Now push it against the surface. You put pressure on the air inside and it escapes under the edge of the cup.

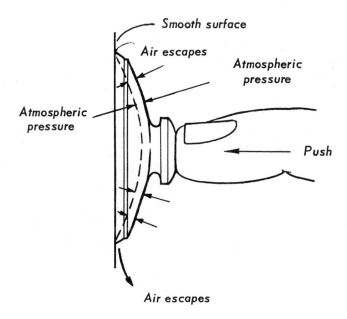

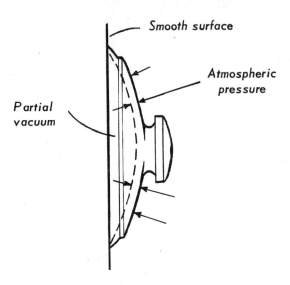

When you stop pushing, the cup springs back to its original shape because it is made of rubber. As it does this a partial vacuum forms inside and the atmospheric pressure holds the cup to the surface.

It's a good idea to coat the bottom edge of the cup to help seal *out* the air. Water works, but soon evaporates. Mineral oil or petroleum jelly will do a good job.

Incidentally, every time I put up a "suction" cup, I think of Otto von Guericke, who performed a very spectacular experiment for the public back in 1650. He made two cups of metal only 22 inches in diameter and, in front of a great crowd of people, put the cups together and pumped out the air from inside them. The crowd couldn't believe its eyes when it took eight horses hitched up to each cup and pulling for all they were worth to finally separate them. Of course, those people in those days didn't know about a vacuum and atmospheric pressure.

Your friends won't believe their eyes either

when you boil water with an ice cube and a vacuum. Willy was a little skeptical until I showed him how to do it.

EXPERIMENT 13

Materials: Glass container for boiling water

Rubber stopper for container

Water

Ice cube

Pot holder

Source of heat

Fill the glass container about one-third full of

Parade

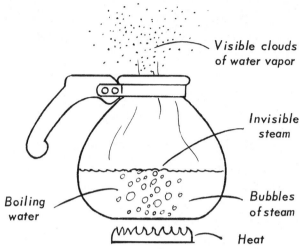

Visible clouds
of water vapor

Invisible
steam

Boiling
water

Bubbles
of steam

Heat

water and put it on the stove to boil. The bottom of
a vacuum coffee maker is fine if you can get a rubber
stopper for the top. When the water is boiling vigorously, it's at 212 degrees Fahrenheit and changing
to steam. You can see the steam rising in the form
of bubbles. The air in the space above the water is
driven out by the steam. When you take the pot off
the stove and put the stopper in place, things begin
to happen.

The pot and its contents begin to cool off. The
water is still very hot but not hot enough to boil. As

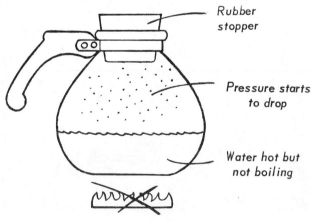

Rubber
stopper

Pressure starts
to drop

Water hot but
not boiling

the steam which filled the space above the water cools, it changes back to water and takes up less space than it did before. A partial vacuum begins to form and we're going to help it form faster by hurrying up the cooling. Turn the pot upside down and place an ice cube on the bottom.

The steam now condenses so fast, the pressure drops quickly. Your friends probably don't realize it, but water boils at a lower temperature when under less than atmospheric pressure. (If you don't realize it either, don't forget about Chapter 12.) You've got a good partial vacuum forming as the

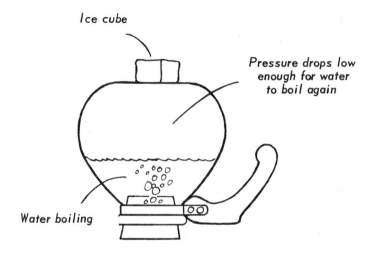

Ice cube

Pressure drops low enough for water to boil again

Water boiling

ice helps to change the steam back to water and that means less pressure. Your friends (and maybe you, too) will be surprised to see the water start boiling again.

Don't let the pot cool off too long or you and your friends will get an even greater surprise. The pressure inside will become so low that the atmospheric pressure will crush the pot with a violent implosion (an implosion is a bursting *in* and an explosion is a bursting *out*).

Some of the same principles that helped you boil water with an ice cube help you make coffee.

EXPERIMENT 14

Materials: **Vacuum coffee maker**

Coffee

Water

Source of heat

(Cups, if desired, for drinking coffee when experiment is over)

Instead of waiting for the coffee to be made, let's watch it while it's being made.

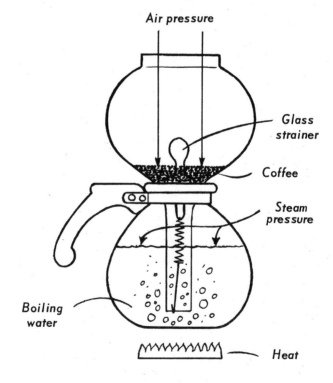

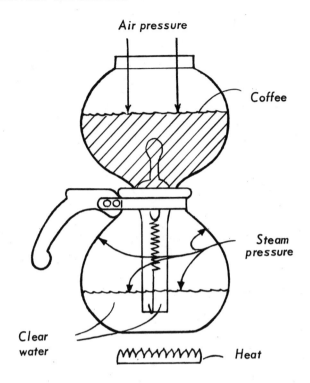

Air pressure

Coffee

Steam pressure

Clear water

Heat

Atmospheric pressure is all around, of course. But we're especially interested in the downward push through the coffee and onto the top of the water in the bottom pot. As the water boils, it changes to steam which takes up more room. Pressure develops and the water is forced up the tube past the strainer to mix with the coffee.

When you turn off the heat, the steam cools off, changes back to water and a partial vacuum forms in the lower section. The atmospheric pressure pushes the water down, the strainer holds back the coffee grounds as the water (now coffee) starts down the tube.

When all the coffee has been pushed back into the lower section, there is a "sucking" noise and bub-

41

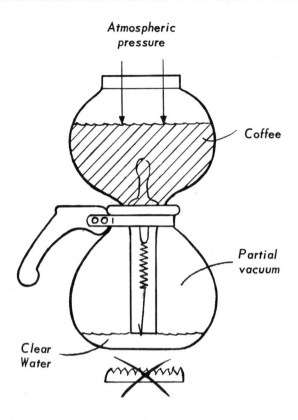

bles come out of the tube. But atmospheric pressure is an old friend by now and you know the bubbling sound is that old friend filling up what's left of the partial vacuum above the coffee.

And if you drink coffee, and got the cups out before, thank that old friend, atmospheric pressure, for helping you make it.

A vacuum helps you in lots of other ways besides making coffee. You should be able to glance around the room and find lots of vacuums (vacua, to be correct) at work.

Can you see a thermos bottle or a vacuum cleaner? How about concentrated fruit juice? The

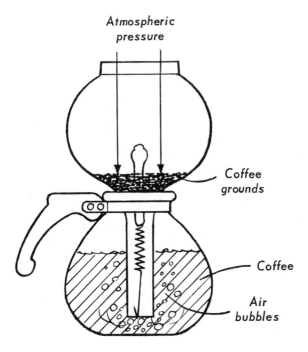

Atmospheric
pressure

Coffee
grounds

Coffee

Air
bubbles

Air pushes in at end of coffee maker,
causing bubbles and gurgling

water in the fresh juice is boiled away in a vacuum to keep the temperature low enough to preserve the flavor and vitamins in the juice. You did the same thing when you boiled water with an ice cube!

The implosion I cautioned you about at the time is harmless but dramatic if done with a gallon tin can!

EXPERIMENT 15

Materials: Gallon tin can with screw top

Pitcher of water

Source of heat

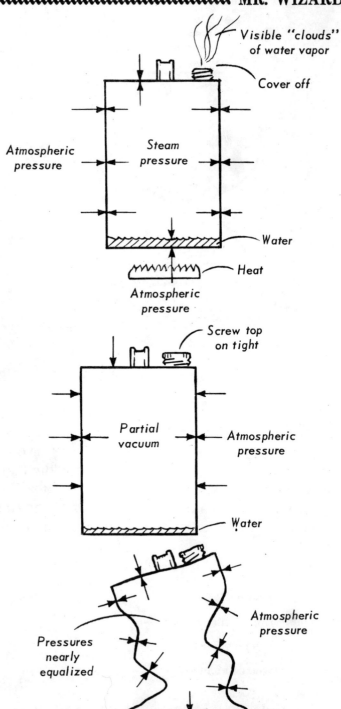

Visible "clouds" of water vapor

Cover off

Atmospheric pressure

Steam pressure

Water

Heat

Atmospheric pressure

Screw top on tight

Partial vacuum

Atmospheric pressure

Water

Pressures nearly equalized

Atmospheric pressure

The can that works best is the rectangular kind that varnish comes in. Remove the screw top, pour in about a half a cup of water and place it on the stove. When you can see wispy clouds of water vapor coming from the top you know this is the situation inside:

All the air has been forced out of the can and the pressure of the steam on the inside balances the pressure of the atmosphere on the outside. When you remove the can from the stove and screw the top on tight this happens:

The steam cools, changes to water, a partial vacuum forms inside and the atmospheric pressure starts to squeeze. You can help the squeezing by pouring cold water over the can to make it cool off faster. With a twisting and groaning the can is crushed by the air until the pressure is nearly equal again.

A hole in the air can be a very useful or damaging thing with atmospheric pressure all around us the way it is. If you don't believe it, look:

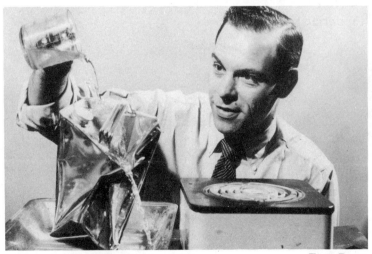

Fran Byrne

Chapter Three

What's burning?

WE HAVEN'T INVESTIGATED air's most important secret. In fact, without this secret ingredient you wouldn't be able to live at all. Let's find out something about it.

EXPERIMENT 16

Materials: Dish of water

Candle in holder

Milk bottle

Matches

Set the candle and holder in the water so that five or six inches of it is above the surface of the water. Now light the candle and hold the milk bottle ready to put over the candle.

When you put the milk bottle over the candle, the candle continues to burn for a short while. However, the flame gets lower and lower and finally goes

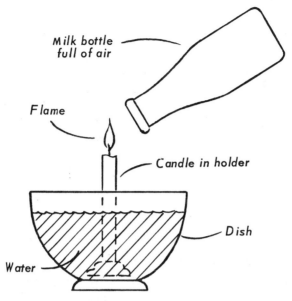

Milk bottle full of air

Flame

Candle in holder

Dish

Water

out and the water in the dish rises into the neck of the milk bottle.

As the candle burned, it united with the secret ingredient of the air: oxygen. When the supply of oxygen in the air in the bottle ran low, the candle went out.

Light the candle and place the funnel over it as

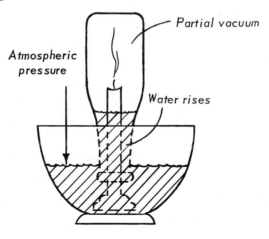

Partial vacuum

Atmospheric pressure

Water rises

you did the milk bottle. Because the funnel has a hole in the top you might expect the candle to burn. However, it goes out just as it did when you put the milk bottle over it!

EXPERIMENT 17

Materials: **Dish of water**

Candle and matches

A large funnel

Piece of tubing

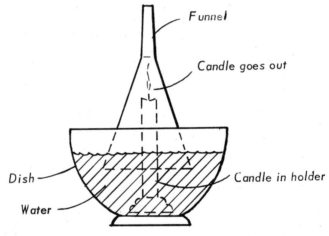

Here's why the candle goes out even though there's a hole in the funnel. When the oxygen in the air inside the funnel combines with the materials in the candle to form a flame, hot gases result which go out the "chimney" of the funnel. While the gases are going up, very little "new" air can come down the "chimney." Unfortunately, by the time the air can get down into the chimney, the candle is out. We've got to bring the air in another hole near the bottom of the candle in order for it to burn. Here's how to do it without punching a hole in the funnel:

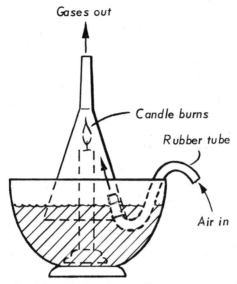

To the inside of the funnel, attach a rubber tube with tape. Make sure that the mouth of the tube is above the level to which the water will come when you put the funnel into the water. Now light the candle and place the funnel over it as before. This time air will be able to go up in the tube around the candle flame, supplying it with the necessary oxygen. The gases go out the chimney at the top as they did before. Incidentally, be sure when you put the funnel and tube into the water that you allow no water to get into the tube because it will block off the passage of air and the candle will go out. Notice that with or without the tube, water does not rise in the funnel as it did in the milk bottle. The reason it doesn't, of course, is because there was no partial vacuum formed by the burning.

What you've actually done with the funnel and the tube is to create a "draft" very much like that in a furnace. There's an opening for "new" air to get to the fire and an opening for the gases to escape.

This happens every time a candle burns—the heat in the flame of the candle sets up currents which supply it continually with oxygen from the air.

That's what all burning is—a chemical process of combining something with oxygen accompanied by heat and light, like this:

Fran Byrne

What I use to make a large flash like that is a special kind of paper treated so that it will burn up completely in a flash. In other words, it combines with the oxygen in the air to form nothing but gases and no ashes at all. It's called flash paper and can be purchased from a magic store. Other materials combine with the oxygen in the air too but not quite so easily as flash paper. Ordinary paper, for instance, burns fairly readily as do some kinds of wood. Coal, on the other hand, is a little harder to get started and steel is harder yet . . . unless you know how to do it. To make steel burn, let's look at paper first. Have you ever put a whole daily newspaper all folded up into a fire? The top few sheets burn quickly but some of the inside sheets may not burn at all because they're not getting enough oxygen. When you crumple paper into a ball all parts of it get more oxygen and it burns easily. You do the same thing with wood but, of course, you can't crumple it so you split it up into kindling. Coal is pretty hard to start, but when you grind it into a powder it burns without any trouble at all. In fact, coal dust in mines can be very dangerous because sometimes explosions result. The same thing is true with steel. If you heat it up enough and give it plenty of oxygen it will burn. Here's how you can burn steel at home.

EXPERIMENT 18

Materials: **Candle in holder**

Matches

Toothpick

Steel wool

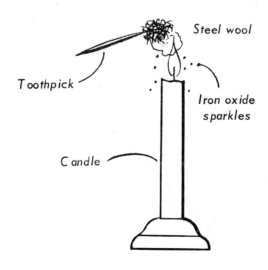

Simply roll up a small quantity of steel wool into a loose bundle on the end of the toothpick. Then hold the steel wool in the candle flame and you'll see tiny sparklers of burning steel fall to the table.

The small sparklers are pieces of steel combining with the oxygen in the air to form a new compound called "iron oxide." You have actually burned steel.

Steel and iron and lots of other things too are often doing a "slow burn" around your house all the time. There's not much heat given off nor any light at all so you don't call it burning. Instead you call it "rusting." "Oxidizing" is a more scientific way of saying the same thing. When iron or steel rusts it combines with the oxygen in the air like the candle did in the milk bottle. Let's do something like we did then and see how much oxygen it takes to rust—or oxidize—steel.

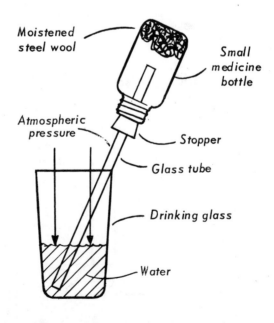

Moistened steel wool

Small medicine bottle

Atmospheric pressure

Stopper

Glass tube

Drinking glass

Water

EXPERIMENT 19

Materials: **Steel wool**

              Medicine bottle

              One-hole rubber stopper to fit bottle

              Glass tubing to fit rubber stopper

              Drinking glass with water in it

Moisten the steel wool with water and place it in the bottom of the medicine bottle. Then put the stopper and tubing into it and set it in the water as shown in the drawing on the opposite page.

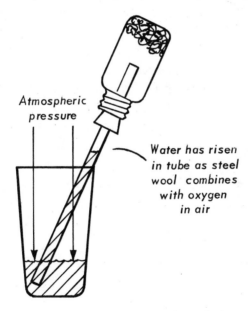

Atmospheric pressure

Water has risen in tube as steel wool combines with oxygen in air

The oxygen in the air inside the bottle will slowly combine with the steel wool to form iron oxide in much the same way as when you burned the steel wool in the candle flame. However, the process will go on much more slowly and you won't be able to see it. But watch the column of water inside the glass tube. As the oxygen in the bottle combines with the steel wool, it no longer takes up as much room as it did before and a partial vacuum will be formed. Atmospheric pressure will push the water into the tube to fill up that partial vacuum and in a day or two your apparatus will look like the drawing on the previous page.

So you see steel will combine with the oxygen in the air if water is present and you give the reaction enough time.

When you want to get rid of a basket full of waste paper you can take it out in the back yard and burn it. Part of the paper changes to a gas that you can't see when it combines with oxygen in the burning process. Wouldn't it be real handy to be able to get rid of an ink spot on a piece of cloth by combining it with oxygen and changing it into a material you can't see? You can't burn it up because you'd burn up the cloth too. Let's do it by using oxygen, not from the air, but from water! You see, water is made up of hydrogen and oxygen so we have a supply of oxygen available in water. Instead of using a cloth to put an ink spot on, let's set up the materials so we can do a magic trick.

EXPERIMENT 20

Materials: Two drinking glasses

Water

Ink

Bleach (like Chlorox)

Fill one glass half full of water and add enough ink to color it. Put a few drops of bleach (like Chlorox) in the bottom of the other glass. To your friends the second glass will look empty. Call attention to the fact that the first glass has "wine" in it.

Just enough ink in ½ glass of water to color it

Few drops of bleach (like Chlorox) in bottom of glass

Then, with the appropriate magic word, "Oxidation," pour the ink water into the other glass. The color will disappear . . . and you've changed "wine" to "water"!

Pour ink water into other glass and color disappears

The trick of changing "wine" to "water" is as old as magic itself—but it's not magic at all. You know oxygen is what does it. How the oxygen gets out of the water is a lot more interesting than the trick. Here's how it happens: the bleach contains the element chlorine which, when added to water, combines with the hydrogen in the water, freeing oxygen. This oxygen combines with the colored material in the ink changing it to a colorless material. You call it "bleaching." But the bleach doesn't really bleach. It combines with hydrogen in the water. The liberated oxygen does the bleaching.

When I wanted to set the flash paper off, I didn't need much heat to get it hot enough to burn. Other materials have to be heated to higher temperatures before they will start to burn. This fact can be used for sending secret messages to your friends. You write with a special kind of ink which disappears. Only your friends who know the secret will be able to make the writing reappear and read your message. Here's what you do:

EXPERIMENT 21

Materials: **Sheets of writing paper**

Clean pen and pen holder

Lemon

"Ink" of vinegar or lemon juice, etc., which, when dry, is invisible

Heavy writing paper

Lemon

Cut the lemon in half and you've got your secret ink well. Jab the clean pen into it until you have plenty of lemon-juice "ink" on the pen. Now, writing with fairly bold strokes, print whatever message you want on the paper. When the lemon juice dries it will be invisible. You can use vinegar, too, but it doesn't work as well as the lemon juice. I showed Willy a blank sheet of paper on which I had written a secret message. When he found out what he had to do to make the writing appear—and did it— here's what he saw:

Ben and Sid Ross

Making the invisible secret writing visible is simple when you know how. Heat the sheet of paper very gently over a candle or a stove. (Careful, don't set the paper on fire!) As the paper and the secret writing begin to heat up, the secret writing starts to combine with oxygen at a lower temperature than the paper does. As the writing combines with oxygen it gets darker and becomes visible. When you've finished heating the message it will look like you wrote it with brown ink—instead of lemon juice.

This experiment shouldn't be surprising to you if you have toast for breakfast. You heat up the slice of bread in the toaster until it's hot enough to combine with the oxygen in the air and become golden-brown toast. If you heat the bread too long, it will combine with too much oxygen and get too brown—and that will be too bad—— burned toast!

Remember you were able to burn steel wool in the candle flame because it got plenty of oxygen. Other things will burn in the same way.

EXPERIMENT 22

Materials: Resin

Cloth

Old salt shaker

Candle

Matches

Put the cloth around the piece of resin and pound the resin to a powder. Then pour it into an old empty salt shaker. Now shake the powdered resin from the salt shaker onto the flame of the candle. You'll be surprised at what happens. If you don't think it's spectacular, look at Betsy when she tried it.

You can hold a large piece of the same resin in the candle flame and nothing much happens. It'll get warm and melt but won't catch on fire easily. Yet the same resin *when powdered* gets plenty of oxygen from the air around it and burns with a flash.

The same thing will happen to flour when the conditions are right. Now, don't worry, the flour sitting in the can on the shelf in the kitchen won't blow up because the conditions aren't right. Here are the right conditions:

EXPERIMENT 23

Materials: Canister or paint can

Candle in holder

Matches

Dry flour

Small funnel

Piece of rubber tubing

Tablespoon

Arrange the equipment like this:

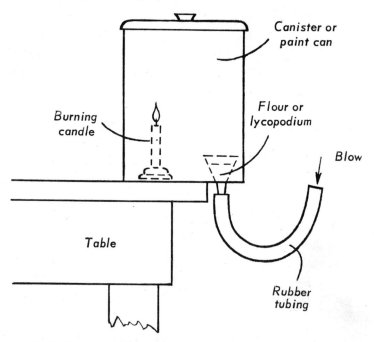

Holding a tablespoon of flour in one hand, light a match with the other and slowly put the burning match right into the flour in the tablespoon. If you expected the flour to burn, it won't. It puts the match out instead, because it shuts off the supply of oxygen to the match. Put the same tablespoon of flour in the funnel in the bottom of the can. Light the candle and place it on the bottom and put the cover on tight. Blow hard into the tube and you've got a spectacular explosion!

Don't worry too much about it though. The explosion isn't very dangerous if you keep your face away from the flame that comes out of the top of the can. Keep an eye on the can cover too. You don't want it to fall on you. Even if it does it can't hurt very much.

Can you understand from your experiment with the resin why you have an explosion when you blow into the tube? The tablespoon of flour didn't burn when you put the match into it because it couldn't get enough air, but when you blew hard into the tube you spread the flour throughout the air inside the can. Each tiny particle has a lot more air (and the oxygen in the air) around it. The flour near the candle flame was heated up enough to burn. This burning heated up more flour, more burned, and so on. All this happened very quickly, of course. The gases formed when the flour burned all at once and blew the cover right off the top of the can.

Burning or combining things with oxygen with heat and light being given off can be helpful or harmful. When the fire is in the furnace, that's good, but when the fire is burning up the house, that's not so good.

How can you control burning? Let's find out what it's all about so you'll be able to prevent harmful fires before they start or help put them out quickly while they're still small.

One way you can put out a fire is to shut off its supply of oxygen. Remember what happened when we put the milk bottle over the candle? You can put out a fire in the same way. Smother it with a rug or a damp cloth or anything that's handy as long as it will shut off the supply of oxygen.

Now if we could shut off a fire's supply of oxygen with something that's invisible, it would look rather strange to see fire go out all of a sudden, wouldn't it? You can do it with no trouble at all.

EXPERIMENT 24

Materials: A sheet of paper

Candle in holder

Matches

Baking soda

Vinegar

Drinking glass

Small piece of cardboard

Make the paper into a trough that will run down to the candle in this way:

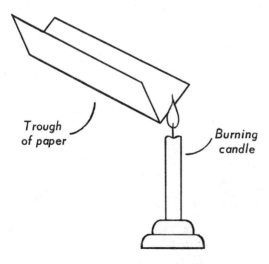

Trough of paper

Burning candle

Now pour half a cup of vinegar into the glass and add a heaping teaspoon of baking soda.

There'll be a chemical reaction in the glass. Wait

Heaping teaspoon
of baking soda

Drinking
glass

Half cup
of vinegar

a few seconds and then cover the glass with the piece
of cardboard. The chemical reaction will fill up the
glass with carbon-dioxide gas. It's invisible so don't

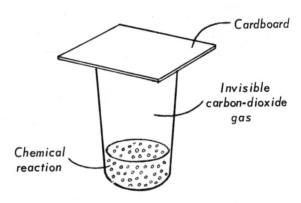

Cardboard

Invisible
carbon-dioxide
gas

Chemical
reaction

bother looking for it. You can put out the candle by
simply pouring the invisible gas (not the liquid)
down the paper trough.

You've shut off the supply of oxygen from
around the candle flame by pouring carbon dioxide
on it. That's why the candle goes out. By the way,
we'll do a lot of other interesting experiments with

64

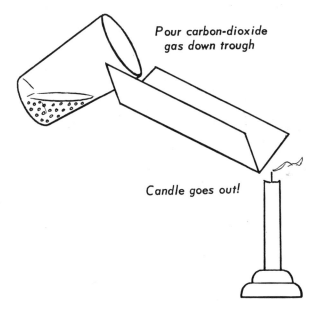

Pour carbon-dioxide gas down trough

Candle goes out!

carbon dioxide in Chapter 14. Firemen make carbon dioxide with special equipment which you'll find out about later.

Now making carbon-dioxide gas and with it putting out fire is fine as long as the fire is on the floor. The gas is heavier than air and sinks to the floor. But what about when the wall's on fire? Let's make bubbles of carbon-dioxide gas in a sticky liquid that firemen can shoot at the wall. It sticks to the wall and smothers the fire. It's called "fire foam."

EXPERIMENT 25

Materials: Licorice extract

Aluminum sulphate

Baking soda

Drinking glasses

Water

Two teaspoons
aluminum
sulphate in
one cup water

Licorice
extract
solution

Make two solutions in the following way: First solution: two tablespoons of aluminum sulphate to one cup of water. Second solution: add licorice extract to about a half cup of baking soda until you get a thick paste. Then to this add an equal amount of water and stir until it's dissolved. When you have the two solutions prepared, pour a little of each at the same time into another glass. Here's what happened when Willy and I did it:

NBC

United Press

The fire foam you see is filled with little bubbles of carbon dioxide. The tough film around each bubble and the carbon dioxide inside smother the fire.

Of course, the best general fire fighter is water, and you should be able to explain why by now. It doesn't smother the fire very much but you know that things burn only when they get hot enough. Remember the paper, wood and coal all have to be heated up to high enough temperatures before they will combine with oxygen or burn. Water cools off the burning building and lowers the temperature to the point where the wood will no longer burn and so the fire goes out. Another reason is that water poured on a fire creates steam, which shuts off oxygen around the flames. It's very important, too, that a good supply of water be available in hydrants ready to be used whenever the firemen need it.

Chapter Four

What makes an airplane fly?

YOU'VE SEEN LOTS OF AIRPLANES up in the sky. Maybe you have even been inside of one as it took off from the ground and climbed high up among the clouds. What makes that airplane fly? You can solve that mystery for yourself with the help of a wood screw and an atomizer!

First, an airplane has to move and that's what the propeller is for. Let's make a propeller that moves.

EXPERIMENT 26

Materials: **Tin from a tin can**

Small tack

Light-weight stick or dowel

Light string or thread

Tin snips or old pair of large scissors

68

Cut a piece of tin from a tin can, pound it flat and, with a pencil, draw a propeller like this on it:

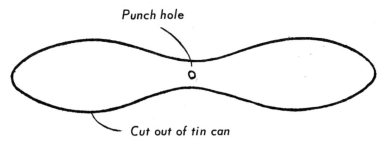

Punch hole

Cut out of tin can

Cut the propeller out and punch a small hole in the center. Then wind the string or thread tightly around one end of a light-weight dowel about 6 inches long. This is to prevent it from splitting when

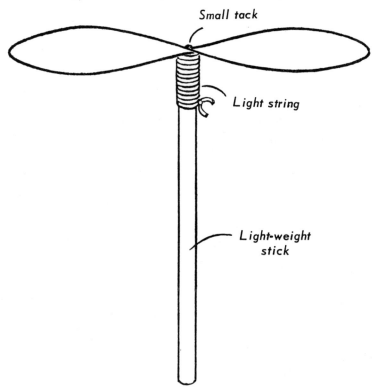

Small tack

Light string

Light-weight stick

you place the propeller on the end of the dowel and fasten it securely with a tack. Twist the blade of the propeller in opposite directions and you're ready to go. Hold the dowel between the palms of your hands. Move one palm forward and the other palm back, twirling the stick and quickly take your hands away.

The propeller will pull itself right over your head. By bending the blades of the propeller to the right angle you can get the propeller to go quite high.

With the help of an ordinary spool you can make a propeller that will go higher yet.

EXPERIMENT 27

Materials: **Spool**

Tin propeller similar to the one in the last experiment

Small brads or finishing nails

Piece of wood for a handle

Knife

Piece of stout string

At one end of the piece of wood carve out a round peg slightly smaller than the hole in the spool and slightly shorter than the length of the spool. Space the two brads evenly between the hole and the outside edge of one end of the spool and pound them down part way. Cut a propeller out of tin as in the previous experiment, but this time punch two holes in it to match the brads in the spool. The holes must be big enough to allow the propeller to slip off the brads easily.

Wind just enough string on the spool so you can pull it all off easily when you hold the flying "ma-

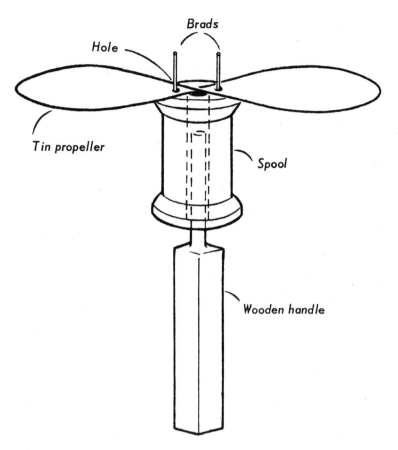

chine" in one hand and pull the string with the other. With the string wound on the spool, place the propeller on the brads and pull the string as fast as you can. This propeller, properly adjusted, will really go high into the air.

Why does a spinning propeller move anyway? For the same reason a wood screw goes into wood when you turn it with a screwdriver. As the threads turn, they pull the screw into the wood. A propeller is really a small portion of the thread of a very large screw.

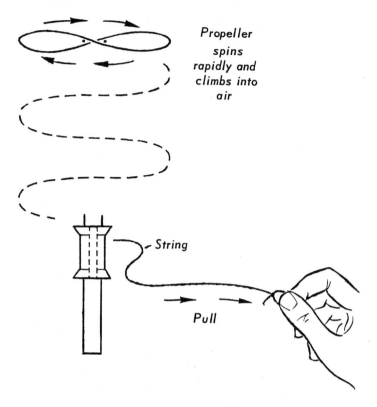

Propeller
spins
rapidly and
climbs into
air

String

Pull

What about a jet plane? It has no propeller. What pulls or pushes it through the air? You'll find your answer in a toy balloon.

EXPERIMENT 28

Materials: Toy balloon

Blow up the balloon and pinch the mouth shut with your fingers. As you blew, you forced air inside the balloon and it pushed against the sides of the balloon making it bigger. The pressure of the air inside the balloon is equal in all directions.

What will happen when you suddenly let go of the neck of the balloon? Let's see *why* it happens

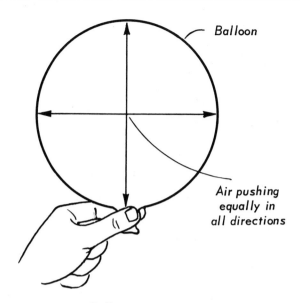

Balloon

Air pushing
equally in
all directions

Balloon moves
this way

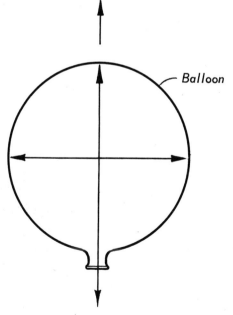

Balloon

Air escapes

before you try it. When you let go, the air inside the balloon is released at the mouth and suddenly the pressures inside the balloon aren't equal in all directions any more. There's a hole where the air inside the balloon can escape instead of pushing. The air pushing against the front of the balloon isn't balanced by the air pushing against the back, so the air in front pushes the balloon forward.

Of course, a jet plane doesn't have a balloon inside of it. It burns special fuel in a special engine that sets up pressures like those inside the balloon. The unbalanced pressure at the front of the jet engine is what drives a jet plane forward.

Why should an airplane move anyway? Seems like a silly question. To go some place, of course. But the fact that a plane *moves* through the air is what keeps it up. You will understand all about that when you have done five little mysteries, all based on the same principle.

Do each one of them and then we'll solve them all at once.

EXPERIMENT 29

Materials: Strip of thin paper about 12 inches long and 2 inches wide

Hold the end of the paper with one finger *under your nose* and blow through your mouth. You expect the paper to rise. The air you blow hits the paper and forces it up as shown in drawing on opposite page.

EXPERIMENT 30

Materials: Same as preceding experiment

Now hold the paper *against your chin* and blow hard. Betsy was surprised when the paper went up.

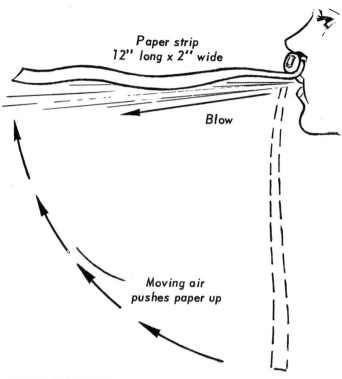

Paper strip
12" long x 2" wide

Blow

Moving air
pushes paper up

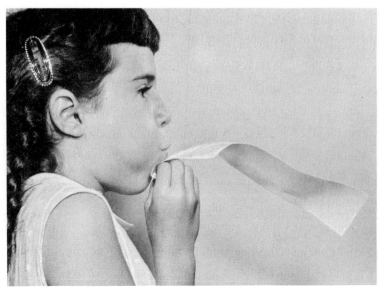

You expected the paper to go up when you blew under it. Why does it go up when you blow *over* it too? That's one of the little mysteries. Here's another:

EXPERIMENT 31

Materials: Sheet of stiff paper or thin cardboard about 4 inches by 8 inches
(A filing card works fine)

Fold the ends of the cardboard over to right angles one inch from each end.

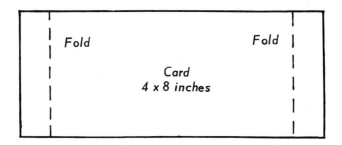

Place the cardboard "arch" on the table and blow hard *under* the arch trying to blow it over.

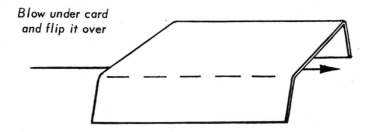

You'll find that the harder you blow, the harder the cardboard sticks to the table. Why can't you blow the cardboard over? When we've solved that mystery we'll know why an airplane flies.

EXPERIMENT 32

Materials: Piece of light cardboard 2 inches square

Straight pin

Spool

Push the pin through the center of the cardboard square.

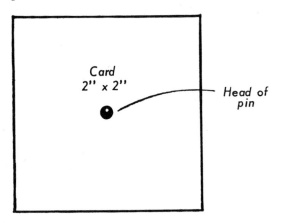

Put the cardboard square on the end of the spool with the pin going into the hole in the spool. The

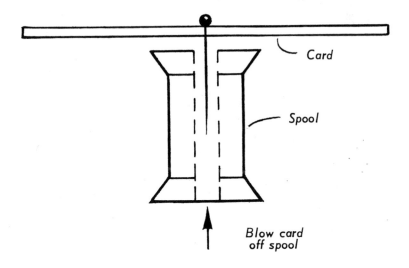

pin keeps the cardboard from moving sideways. Holding the spool with the cardboard aimed at the ceiling, blow through the other end of the spool. See if you can make the cardboard square hit the ceiling.

You'll find you can't blow the cardboard square off the spool no matter how hard you try. Why?

EXPERIMENT 33

Materials: Two sheets of writing paper

When you blow down between the sheets of paper, a surprising thing happens. Instead of being blown apart, as you would expect, the sheets come together.

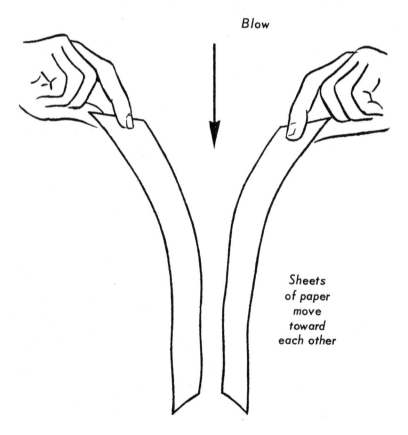

Blow

*Sheets
of paper
move
toward
each other*

EXPERIMENT 34

Materials: **Vacuum cleaner with hose for attachments**

Balloon with wire weight

Table-tennis ball

Blow up the balloon, tie it off and add enough wire to weight it. With the hose attached to the *blower* end, turn on the vacuum cleaner and hold the hose straight up. Carefully place the table-tennis ball in the middle of the stream of air. The air coming out of the hose pushes up on the table-tennis ball hard enough to hold it suspended in mid air. Place the balloon above the ball in the air stream. It will be suspended in mid-air too.

Toivo Kaitila

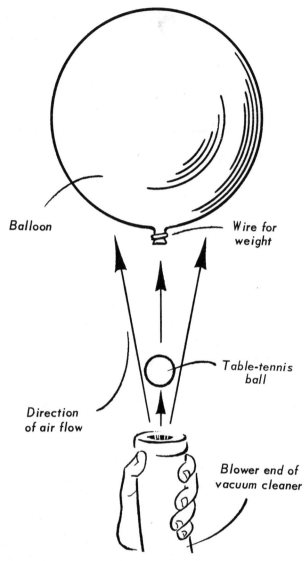

Balloon

Wire for weight

Table-tennis ball

Direction of air flow

Blower end of vacuum cleaner

Now, why don't the table-tennis ball and the balloon roll off to the side of the column of air and then fall down? You can even move the mouth of the hose slowly from side to side and the table-tennis ball and the balloon will move with it. What holds them in the middle of the stream of air? If you are puzzled, don't worry. Willy was too when he tried it.

Now, let's solve all these mysteries at once . . . with an atomizer!

EXPERIMENT 35

Materials: **Two glass tubes**

Drinking glass half full of water

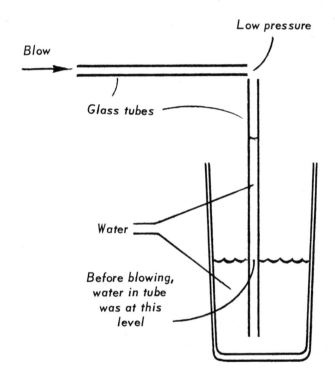

Blow

Low pressure

Glass tubes

Water

Before blowing, water in tube was at this level

Place one glass tube into the water in the glass and the other at right angles so the ends of the tubes are close together. Now blow into the horizontal tube.

Before you started blowing, the level of the

water in the vertical glass tube was the same as the water in the glass because atmospheric pressure pushed down on the water in the tube as well as on the water in the glass. When you blow through the horizontal tube the air moving across the top of the vertical tube can't push down as hard. An area of low pressure or partial vacuum forms at the top of the vertical tube. Atmospheric pressure on the water in the glass pushes down and forces the water up the vertical tube to fill up the low-pressure area. When the air is moved by squeezing a rubber ball instead of blowing, perfume is used instead of water, and the length of the vertical tube is adjusted so the perfume is pushed all the way up to meet and be scattered by the moving air . . . then you have a perfume atomizer. What's a perfume atomizer got to do with why an airplane flies?

First, let's see how an area of low pressure solves the five little mysteries and then the big mystery of what makes an airplane fly. In each of the five little mysteries you speeded the air up by blowing or by using the blower end of a vacuum cleaner. The pressure of the air (atmospheric pressure) trying to fill up the area of lowered pressure is what made the paper rise, the card stick to the table, the cardboard stay on the end of the spool, the papers go together, and the table-tennis ball and the balloon to stay in the air stream.

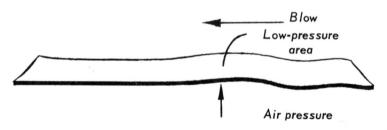

Blow

Low-pressure area

Air pressure

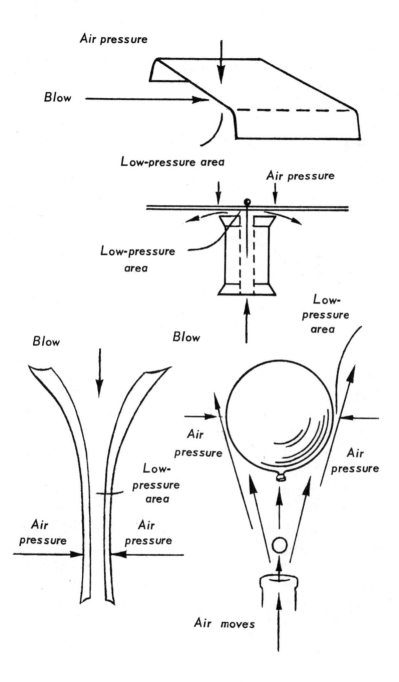

Air pressure

Blow

Low-pressure area

Air pressure

Low-pressure area

Blow

Blow

Low-pressure area

Air pressure

Air pressure

Low-pressure area

Air pressure

Air pressure

Air moves

Now we're ready to solve the big mystery of what makes an airplane fly.

You found out how a propeller or a jet engine moves an airplane through the air. The air flows past all the parts of the airplane just as though the plane were standing still and a giant were blowing in front of it. Let's pretend to cut a wing in half as the plane is flying and see what's going on around it. We are going to investigate this part of the airplane right here.

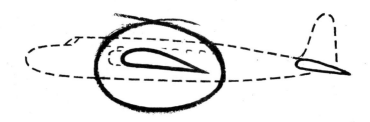

Let's get closer to the cross section of the wing and imagine you can see how the air flows around it. (Remember the airplane is *pulled* through the air by the propeller; the propeller doesn't blow the air over the wing.)

When you held the strip of paper under your nose and blew through your mouth, the paper went up as the air hit it. The same thing happens to the bottom side of the wing as it moves through the air. The air hits it and forces it up. You feel the same force when you are riding in a car and put your hand out of the window. When you hold your hand at about the same angle as the wing is attached to the airplane, your hand is forced up by the air. About one-third of the force necessary to hold the plane in the air comes from the moving air hitting the bottom of the wing.

84

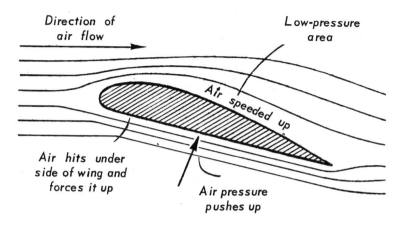

Direction of
air flow

Low-pressure
area

Air speeded up

Air hits under
side of wing and
forces it up

Air pressure
pushes up

Now let's look at what's happening along the top of the wing. The wing is shaped in such a way that the air blowing over the top has further to go and so is speeded up. By now you know what happens when air is speeded up. An area of low pressure forms. The atmospheric pressure pushes up under the wing trying to fill up that lowered-pressure area and, in so doing keeps the airplane up. About two-thirds of the force necessary to hold the plane in the air comes from the air pressure trying to flow to the area of lowered pressure.

Why not see for yourself how it works by making a wing section out of paper?

Paste the ends of the strip of paper together like this:

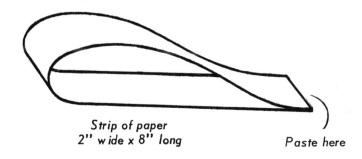

Strip of paper
2" wide x 8" long

Paste here

EXPERIMENT 36

Materials: **Strip of writing paper about 2 inches wide and 8 inches long**

A dab of paste or glue

Pencil

Place your paper wing on the pencil and blow *across the top*. The same thing will happen to your wing as happens to a real one; it will "fly." Don't forget, you're making the air flow over the wing by blowing. The air really flows over the airplane wing because the plane is moving through the air, pulled by the propeller or pushed by a jet engine.

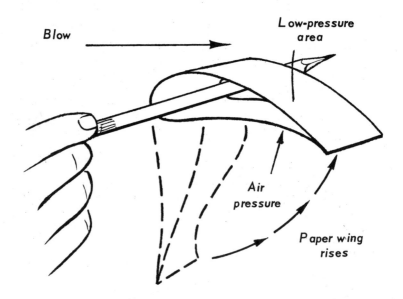

So you see, we solved, with a wood screw and an atomizer, all the five little mysteries and the big mystery of what makes an airplane fly.

Chapter Five

Why balance gets lost

WHAT IS "UP," ANYWAY? The easiest answer for you, probably, is to point your finger to the sky and say, "That's up." But if you continued that same direction down through the earth until you came out on the other side, you'd be pointing down! So "up" is a direction, all right, but with some qualifications. Let's look at what some of those qualifications are.

"Up" is the opposite of "down." Nobody will argue about that. "Down" is the direction things move when they fall. In other words, things are pulled toward the earth by the force of gravity and the direction in which they move is "down." "Up" being the opposite of "down" means "up" is *away from the earth*. That's why you point your finger at the sky and say, "That's up." Just so it will be clear in your mind you can do a very simple experiment.

EXPERIMENT 37

Materials: **Grapefruit**

Toothpicks

Plunge the toothpicks into the grapefruit at different points. Where you put them really doesn't matter as long as they stick out straight. The other end of each toothpick will be pointing "up." So the answer to the question of "What is up?" is, "Up is away from the earth; down is toward the earth." The reason for the difference between up and down is the force of gravity. Let's look at it.

But you can't see the force of gravity. However, you can see what the force of gravity does, so you'll have to investigate that.

You know the force of gravity pulls you toward the earth. Doesn't it sound logical to assume that the heavier an object is, the faster it will be pulled toward the earth? A long time ago many people thought so. Then a man by the name of Galilei Galileo, who did many experiments in many fields of science, did an amazing thing. He proved it wasn't so. This is the way he did it:

EXPERIMENT 38

Materials: **Grapefruit**

Orange

Hold the grapefruit and the orange in front of you at about eye level so that they are at the same height. Then let go of them both at the same time. Which will hit the floor first, the grapefruit or the orange? Here's what happened when Betsy tried it.

Which hit first, the grapefruit or the orange? If both started falling at the same time, they both

hit the floor at the same time! That's why you probably had trouble telling which one hit first.

This simple experiment is important for several reasons. When Galileo first did it, it showed that the people who believed that the heavier an object was the faster it would fall, were wrong. And secondly, it pointed out the importance of proving by trying—by experiment—the ideas people had about the world around them. Previous to that time many philosophers only thought and talked about the things around them without actually looking and trying experiments. Galileo, however, did many experiments and *proved* with them that the conclusions he came to actually fit the facts. He didn't use a grapefruit and an orange when he did the experiment you and Betsy did. He used metal balls of different weights and is supposed to have dropped them from a leaning tower in the town of Pisa, Italy. Here's a picture of it.

The leaning tower of Pisa, like Galileo's experiment, is interesting for two reasons too. First, you can imagine Galileo standing on the balcony dropping the light ball and the heavy ball and the amazement of the people when they saw them both hit the ground at the same time. Secondly, as you look at the tower you will notice that it is leaning over quite far! Why doesn't it fall over? Before we're through investigating the force of gravity, you'll understand why the leaning tower of Pisa continues to lean and not to fall.

Before we do that, however, let's do another experiment like dropping the grapefruit and the orange but this time get different results.

EXPERIMENT 39

Materials: Small balls of cotton

Thread

Small sheets of tin or aluminum foil

Make little balls of cotton as nearly the same size as you can. Cut out from a sheet of tin or aluminum foil, two identical squares. With the thread tie the cotton balls to the sheets of tin foil, like this:

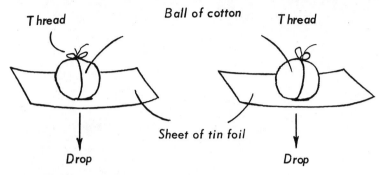

Thread   Ball of cotton   Thread

Sheet of tin foil

Drop   Drop

Hold the two sheets of tin foil with the cotton on top of them about eye level and drop them at the same time as you did the grapefruit and the orange. Which hits the ground first?

Both will probably hit at pretty close to the same time as you would expect from your previous experiment. Now do this, however. Leave one of the cotton balls and tin foil just as it is. Take the other one and roll the tin foil around the piece of cotton so that you have a little ball with cotton inside and tin foil around the outside.

Now hold them both at eye level and drop them, as you did before. Which one hits first? This time

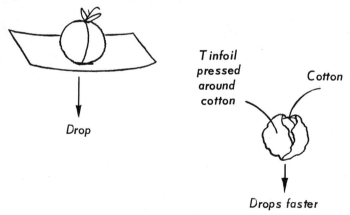

Drop

Tinfoil pressed around cotton

Cotton

Drops faster

you will find that the little ball of cotton and tin foil will hit the floor first. You have added no weight. Are you defying the laws of gravity? Not at all, because you have to take something else into consideration this time.

Remember in Chapter 1 we found that the air was like an ocean and you're living at the bottom of it? Well, if you drop an object in the ocean you can understand how the water has to flow around it as it falls to the bottom. The air, too, has to flow around an object that moves through it. The moving object has to push the air out of the way. Because both pieces of foil and cotton weigh the same, gravity is pulling them down with the same force. The flat piece has a lot of air to push out of the way while the rolled-up piece has little air to push out of the way—*because* it's rolled up. That's why the rolled-up piece hits the floor first. It's sort of streamlined to reduce air resistance.

You could prove it's the resistance of the air that makes the difference by dropping both pieces in a vacuum. If you did, you'd find that they'd both fall at exactly the same rate. However, a vacuum good enough to do that sort of experiment is pretty hard to make at home, so here's another way of doing it.

EXPERIMENT 40

Materials: **A book**

A sheet of paper a little smaller than the cover of the book

Place the paper on top of the book so that none of the edges of the paper stick out over the edge of the book. Then hold the book up about eye level and drop both the paper and the book at the same time. You will notice that they stay together all the way down which means that they must drop at the same rate. You see, here's what happens:

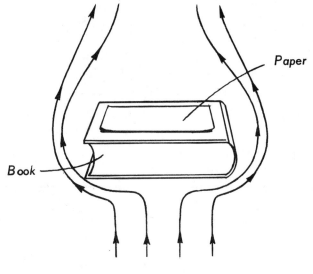

Air flows

As the book falls through the air, the air is pushed aside as indicated by the arrows. That means that the light-weight paper that would ordinarily flutter to the ground has the air pushed out of the way in front of it by the book. The paper can now drop as fast as the book does. That's why both the book and the paper hit the floor at the same time.

While the book's there on the floor, step back one full step. Pick up the book. Here's Willy trying it:

Willy couldn't pick up the book without falling over and you won't be able to either. Why?

Here's another puzzle: how could you balance a cork and two forks on the point of a needle?

Ben and Sid Ross

The solution of the puzzle of how to balance two forks and a cork on the point of a needle is really another puzzle. Why do the cork and the two forks stay balanced on the point of the needle? To understand why, you have to play with blocks. Here's what Willy and I used to solve the puzzle of why he couldn't pick up the book and why the cork and two forks balanced on the point of a needle. You can make your own equipment out of anything around the house.

EXPERIMENT 41

Materials: **A block of wood**

Some tacks

A hammer

Some string

Into at least three of the sides of the block of wood pound a tack part of the way into the wood. Next tie the string to the head of the tack and hold the block of wood up so it can hang freely.

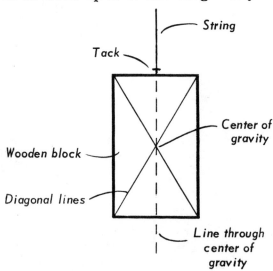

Notice that the block of wood comes to rest in a position that depends on where you put the tack. If you pretend to draw a line straight down from the string it would look like the dotted one in the drawing. Now put the string on one of the other tacks and hang the block up again. If you pretend to draw a line straight down from the string, this second imaginary line will cross the first one someplace inside of the block of wood.

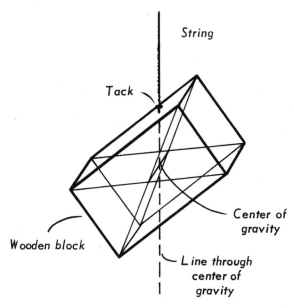

String

Tack

Center of gravity

Wooden block

Line through center of gravity

The place where the two imaginary lines cross is called the center of gravity of the block because that is where the force of gravity seems to be pulling on the block.

Now hang the block up by a third tack. Pretend to draw a line straight down from the string and you'll find the third imaginary line goes right through the other two at the center of gravity! What are we trying to prove with the hanging

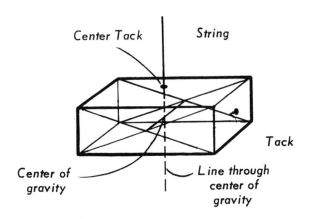

block and all these imaginary lines? Simply this: that when an object is held up at only one point the force of gravity will automatically line up the center of gravity of the object directly under the point of support. No matter where you put the tack and string, when you hold the block up by the string the center of gravity is directly under the string. Why do we want to know about the center of gravity? Because it's important to understanding why you can't pick up the book without falling over and why the cork and two forks balance on the point of a needle. But we've got to do one other experiment before we can understand those two puzzles.

EXPERIMENT 42

Materials: **Block used in the above experiment**

Same string

A small weight

A table

A piece of wood four or five times as long as the block

Put a tack on one of the large surfaces of the

block directly above the center of gravity. To this tack, tie the string, and at the other end of the string tie a weight. Then put the piece of wood on the edge of the table and place the block near the center of the wood so that the weight hanging from the string can hang over the edge of the table. Now pick up the piece of wood and slowly raise one end of it.

How high will you have to raise the piece of wood before the block will fall? Notice that as long as the vertical line through the center of gravity (represented by the string with the weight on it) falls within the base of the block, the block does not fall.

But as you gradually raise the piece of wood, note what happens when the string moves outside the base of the block. As soon as the vertical line

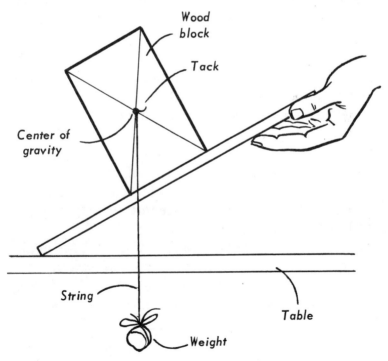

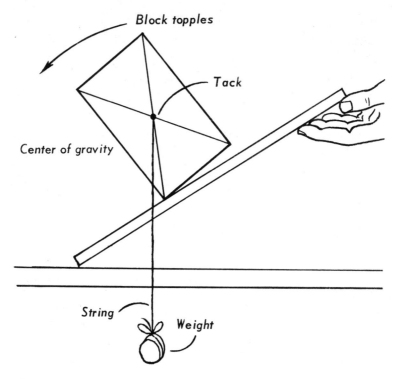

through the center of gravity falls outside the base of the block, the block topples over.

The two experiments you have just done can be summed up like this: any object will be at rest or balanced when it is suspended from a point directly above or below its center of gravity, and an object will remain at rest or balanced as long as the vertical line through its center of gravity remains within the area supporting it.

Now look at the leaning tower of Pisa again. A vertical line through its center of gravity evidently lies within the base of the tower. That's why the leaning tower of Pisa continues to lean and not to fall.

Now can you understand why you can't pick up

the book when you toss it on the floor and take one step back from it? Your center of gravity is somewhere in your midsection, probably somewhere between your hips or a little higher. You have no trouble balancing yourself as long as the vertical line through your center of gravity remains over your base—your feet. But the minute you try to lean forward your center of gravity is going to start moving because you are bending. You automatically take care of this shifting of your center of gravity by moving your hips back so that your center of gravity still remains over your feet.

When you try to lean over further yet, however, the vertical line through your center of gravity gradually moves forward more and more until it is no longer within the area of your feet. At that point

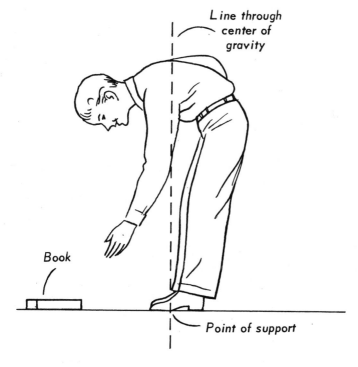

Line through center of gravity

Book

Point of support

you lose your balance and fall forward. So when you lose your balance, you "lose" the vertical line through your center of gravity!

The clowns with the big feet at the circus can lean very far because they wear enormously long shoes. They can lean over further than you can because the vertical line through their center of gravity remains within their long base.

The center of gravity of the block was an imaginary point inside the block and most of the time your center of gravity is inside you. But sometimes it can be outside of the thing that's balanced. When you balanced the cork and the two forks on the needle, the center of gravity actually was not in the cork *or* the forks! As soon as you balance them on the pencil, you know the vertical line through the

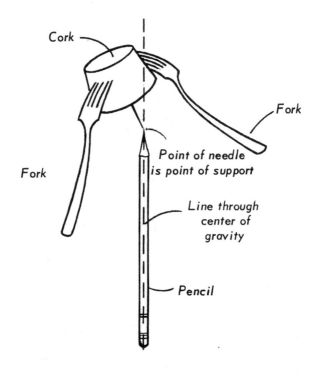

Cork

Fork

Fork

Point of needle
is point of support

Line through
center of
gravity

Pencil

center of gravity must go through the point of support. The center of gravity of the forks, cork and needle must be below the point of support . . . inside the pencil! If you think the center of gravity is above the point of support, try putting the needle in the other end of the cork and balancing them. You'll find it very difficult to keep the vertical line through the center of gravity going through such a small point of support. The whole thing will fall, so get your hands out of the way. You don't want to be jabbed by the needle!

With the center of gravity *below* the point of support, the cork and forks are so well balanced you can gently push one of the forks and the whole thing will spin—on the point of the needle!

Here's a rocking pencil and knife based on the same idea.

EXPERIMENT 43

Materials: A wooden pencil

A pocket knife

Open the large blade of the pocket knife so that it forms a right angle to the handle. (Careful, don't cut yourself.) Push the point of the blade into the pencil near the sharpened end. Balance the pencil and the knife near the edge of the table so the handle of the knife can go under the edge of the table.

Can you find the point of support? That should be easy: the point of the pencil. Can you find the center of gravity? That shouldn't be too hard either because you know that it must lie above or below the point of support because the knife and the pencil are balanced. In this case, because of the weight of the knife, you can assume that the center of grav-

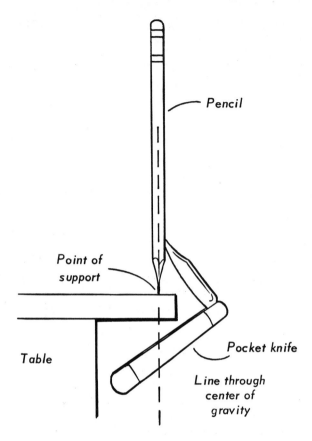

Pencil

Point of
support

Table

Pocket knife

Line through
center of
gravity

ity is probably someplace in the handle of the knife. When you have the pencil balanced you can give the knife a gentle shove and both the pencil and the knife will rock back and forth with ease.

Remember Humpty Dumpty who fell off the wall and couldn't be put together again by all the king's horses and all the king's men? That's what Betsy thought of when she saw an egg peering over the edge of the table.

When Betsy wanted to know why Humpty Dumpty didn't fall, I told her how to make one for herself. You can make one for yourself, too, and

when you've made it, why it doesn't fall will be clear
to you.

EXPERIMENT 44

Materials: **Fresh egg**

> **Pin**

> **Candle**

> **Paper funnel**

> **BB shot**

    With the pin puncture a small hole in both ends
of an egg. Then blow hard in one hole, holding the
other hole over a cup. This will force the contents
of the egg into the cup. Keep the holes as small as
you can and still get the contents of the egg out by
blowing. It may take you a little while to do this.

    When you have emptied the egg, fill one of the
holes with wax from a lighted candle.

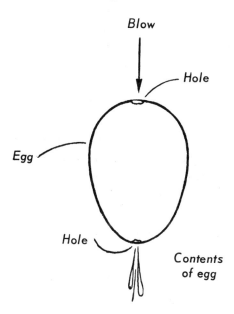

Blow

Hole

Egg

Hole

Contents
of egg

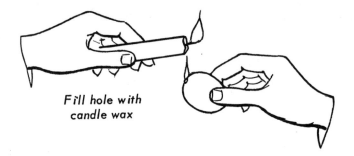

Fill hole with
candle wax

Then fashion a small paper funnel to fit in the other hole and drop in the BB shot until the egg feels fairly heavy when you pick it up.

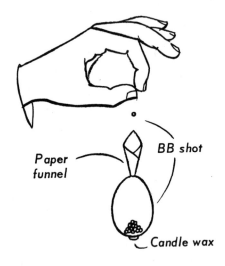

Paper
funnel

BB shot

Candle wax

Then close the remaining hole with wax from the candle. Draw a face on the egg with a crayon and balance your Humpty Dumpty near the edge of the table.

You can see now why your Humpty Dumpty peers over the edge of the table without falling off. Ordinarily the center of gravity of an egg is some-where in the middle of the yolk. When you took the contents of the egg out and put in the BB shot you

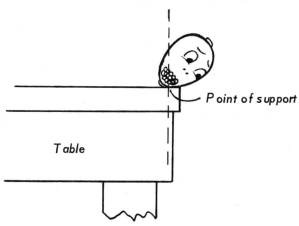

Line through center of gravity

Point of support

Table

lowered the center of gravity. As long as the new center of gravity lies over the table, all the king's horses and all the king's men can forget about putting Humpty Dumpty together again. He won't fall.

When you make a can that rolls away from you only to roll back, then you are using a lowered center of gravity to wind up a rubber band. Here's how to do it.

EXPERIMENT 45

Materials: **Coffee can and cover**

Long, stout rubber band

String

A weight

Punch two holes in the top and bottom of the coffee can. Run the rubber band through the holes and tie it on one side. Where the rubber band crosses, tie the weight securely.

When you roll the can away from you on the floor, the weight will remain below the point of support. The weight winds up the rubber band as the

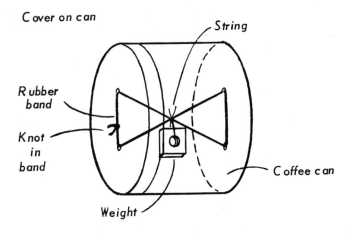

Cover on can

String

Rubber band

Knot in band

Weight

Coffee can

can rolls. When the force you have used to roll the can forward has wound up the rubber band as tight as it will go, the can will slowly begin to roll back and end up right where you started it! To your friends who don't understand about the lowered center of gravity and can't see the rubber bands inside the can, it will look like a very mysterious can indeed. Once they're properly amazed at your skill, pull off the top of the can, show them the weight and explain how the can rolls back. It's all because of that imaginary point called the center of gravity.

Chapter Six

Getting warm

THE TEMPERATURE on the surface of the sun is about 11,000 degrees Fahrenheit. You'd think the closer you got to the sun, the hotter you'd get. Yet, if you've ever flown in an airplane, you know that when you get just a few thousand feet away from the earth it gets pretty cold. Something's funny someplace, and it's in the way you think about the heat of the sun.

You see, the heat from the sun is radiant energy, or tiny, tiny bundles of energy that move in waves. This energy goes right through transparent things like air or glass. But once it hits something opaque it's changed to heat energy and has a hard time going through things like air or glass. Thus, the radiant energy from the sun doesn't heat the air directly. The energy hits the ground, is changed to heat which warms the ground and the ground then warms the air. That's why it's warm near the earth where we live and cold a few thousand feet above us.

A greenhouse has a glass roof to let the radiant energy from the sun in to help plants grow. The radiant energy, of course, goes right through the glass. But once it hits the plants and the ground inside the greenhouse, it is changed to heat energy and can't go back through the glass easily. For this reason the air inside the greenhouse is almost always hotter than the air outside the greenhouse.

You can prove how radiant energy goes through transparent things and is changed to heat energy once it hits an opaque object, if you have a miniature sun. You can buy a miniature sun in the drug store. Just ask the clerk for an infrared lamp. It's not really a miniature sun but it does send out radiant energy like the sun does. Why not change some of the energy from an infrared light bulb to heat energy and pop popcorn in cellophane?

EXPERIMENT 46

Materials: Infrared bulb in socket

Clear cellophane

Embroidery hoops

Popcorn

Salt and butter (not absolutely necessary)

Cut two circles out of the cellophane slightly larger than the embroidery hoops. Open the embroidery hoops and lay one of the rings on the table. Over this lay one of the circles of cellophane. Pour enough popcorn on the cellophane to cover the area. Then lay the other circle of cellophane on top of the popcorn and on top of it all lay the other ring of the embroidery hoop. Press down on the embroidery

hoop and you will have the popcorn imprisoned between two layers of cellophane. Now hold the popcorn in front of the infrared bulb, turn on the bulb
and wait for the corn to pop. Because I've got ring
stands in my home laboratory, Willy and I used one
of them to hold the embroidery hoop and the infrared
bulb in place.

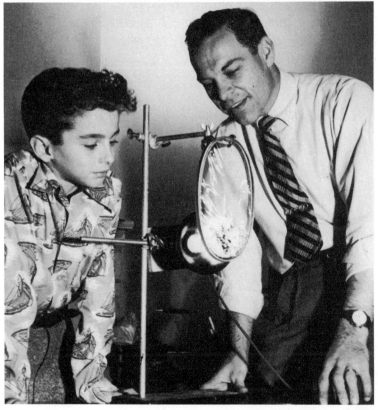

Archie Lieberman—Time

Can you see the popcorn between the sheets of
the cellophane? If you think cellophane won't burn,
hold a lighted match to a small piece of it. It burns,
all right! The cellophane isn't heated up much by

the infrared bulb because the radiant energy from the bulb goes right through it. But when the radiant energy hits a kernel of popcorn it's changed to heat energy and the heat pops the popcorn. In a few minutes you'll have fresh popcorn that needs only butter and salt to be just right.

That's one way of getting warm . . . block radiant energy and it's changed to heat.

There are other ways of getting warm. One way is to conduct the heat from where it is to where you want it like this:

EXPERIMENT 47

Materials: A handkerchief

A coin

A burning cigarette or incense stick

Place the coin under a handkerchief and roll the handkerchief tightly around the coin. Be sure to stretch it tightly over the surface of the coin.

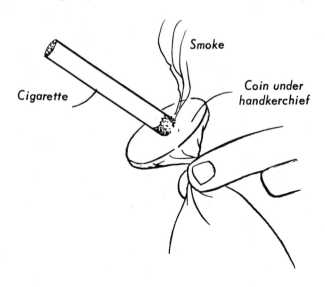

Smoke

Cigarette

Coin under handkerchief

What will happen when you bring the end of the burning cigarette or incense against the cloth? It won't burn a hole in it, if that's what you expected. If you want to prove to someone that you haven't fire-proofed the handkerchief, you can do the same thing without the coin. You'll burn a hole in the handkerchief so you'd better do it with a piece of old cloth. The coin seems to make the difference between burning and not burning a hole in the cloth, but why?

Remember you found in Chapter 3 that things have to be heated up to a certain temperature before they begin to burn. Heat is carried from the cigarette or the incense to the handkerchief and through the handkerchief to the coin. Most metals carry or "conduct" heat a lot better than cloth does. ("Conduct" comes from the Latin word meaning "to lead.") The heat from the cigarette or incense is conducted to all parts of the coin so easily and quickly that not much of it stops to heat up the cloth. The cloth, therefore, is kept below the temperature at which it will start to burn.

By doing the same thing in a different way you can actually *see* how a good conductor of heat can keep something from burning.

EXPERIMENT 48

Materials: **Piece of wire screen**

Candle

Matches

Light the candle and hold the piece of screen about midway in the candle flame.

The candle flame burns below but not above the screen. Here again the heat in the candle flame is

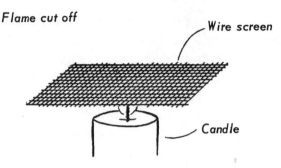

Flame cut off

Wire screen

Candle

conducted away so quickly and easily by the metal
screen that there's not enough heat left to keep the
gases burning above the screen. In order for the
gases to burn above the screen you'll have to get
them hot enough to burn again. You can do this by
lighting the gases that are coming through the screen
with a match.

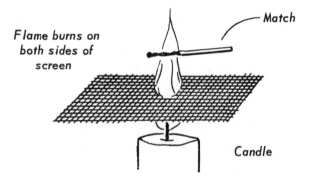

*Flame burns on
both sides of
screen*

Match

Candle

Now the candle flame will burn on both sides of
the screen. You can prove for yourself that most
metals are good conductors of heat by feeling the
heat in a copper wire and a piece of wood.

EXPERIMENT 49

Materials: Copper wire

A match

Cut off a piece of copper wire the same length as the match. Then light the match and hold the copper wire in the flame.

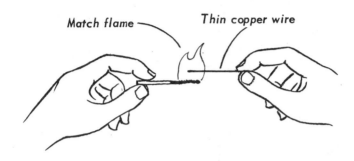

Match flame —⟍   Thin copper wire

Be prepared to drop the wire because it's going to get hot fast. The heat from the match flame will be conducted by the wire to your fingers and you won't be able to feel any heat in the wood of the match because wood is a poor conductor of heat.

Puzzle—find the wooden heat insulators or poor conductors of heat:

When you step out of the bathtub onto the tile floor, your feet feel cold so you hop to the bath mat. But both the tile floor and the bath mat have been in the room for a long time and both are at the same temperature. Why does the tile feel so much colder to your feet than the bath mat? If you had to pick the good conductor of heat, which would it be, the tile floor or the bath mat? The one that carries or conducts the heat away from your foot the fastest is the good conductor—the tile floor, of course. Try putting one foot on the floor and the other on the bath mat and feel the difference between a good and poor conductor of heat.

Which is warmer, two three-pound wool blankets or one six-pound one? Both are made of about

116

the same amount of wool. Here's a clue to the answer. Air is not a very good conductor of heat. That should be enough of a clue for you to figure out that two three-pound blankets are warmer than one six-pound blanket. Between the two three-pound blankets is a thin layer of air, a poor conductor of heat. Therefore, the heat from your body under the blankets is kept under the blankets too, and you feel warm. However, a six-pound wool blanket is plenty warm. What's doing the insulating then? Still partly air. You see, each little fiber of wool has tiny little air spaces inside of it. You can see such air spaces in highly magnified fibers of wool.

Air is such a poor conductor of heat, especially when it's still, that it's used around the house as insulation. Sometimes it's called dead-air space, and you can find it right in the walls of your house. When the carpenters built your house they left a space filled with air between the outside wall and the inside wall. This acts as insulation to keep the heat in during the winter and the heat out in the summer. Around the windows and doors, however, there is no dead-air space, so we make one with storm windows.

Sometimes insulation other than dead air is used in building a house. Some of this material is puffy and an especially poor conductor of heat. You probably won't have any around the house, nor would it be a good idea for you to put a blowtorch one inch away from the back of your hand, so just watch while I do that very thing to Betsy's hand. But *please*, don't try this! It is much too dangerous for a home experiment!

When Betsy put her hand on the table I covered

her hand with a one-inch layer of insulating material. Then, on the center of the pile of insulating material, I placed an ordinary penny. With a blowtorch I heated up the penny and the insulation. The flame of the blowtorch is about 2200 degrees Fahrenheit, yet Betsy didn't feel a thing. To show Betsy how much heat there was right on top of her hand, I touched a match to the penny.

The match burst into flame immediately. That's how hot the penny was. And yet Betsy felt no heat at all. That's how good modern insulation is.

Now you know when you're getting warm by conduction you conduct heat to where you want it by using good conductors, usually metals. And to keep heat from moving where you don't want it, you use poor conductors or insulators, like still air, wood, asbestos, glass, etc. But you can get warm in another way too. You'll see how when you do this:

118

EXPERIMENT 50

Materials: **Two milk bottles**

Cold water

Hot water

Ink

Piece of waxed paper or cardboard

Fill one bottle with clear, cold water. Fill the other bottle with hot water and add enough ink to darken it.

Clear cold water

Hot water

Enough ink to darken water

Clear cold water

Wax paper or card

Over the top of the bottle with the clear, cold water in it, place the waxed paper or cardboard. Then, holding your hand firmly on the cardboard, turn the bottle upside down.

119

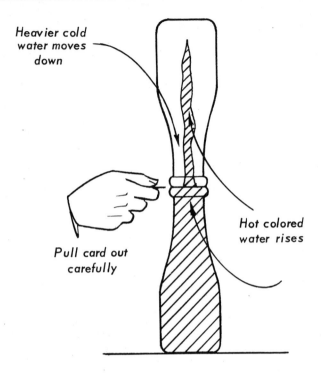

Heavier cold
water moves
down

Pull card out
carefully

Hot colored
water rises

Now place the bottle of clear, cold water carefully on top of the bottle of hot, colored water so that their mouths are one above the other. Slowly remove the waxed paper or cardboard. Right before your eyes the hot, colored water will rise up into the cold, clear water!

What's this got to do with gettin' warm? Well, you'll see. When things are heated up they expand. You can't see water expand as it's heated up because it doesn't expand very much, but it expands enough to make hot water weigh less than an equal volume of cold water. Now can you see why the hot water went up? The clear, cold water is heavier than the warm, colored water so the force of gravity is going to pull down harder on the cold water than on the hot. As gravity pulls the cold, clear water down, the hot, colored water is forced up. Before long both bottles will be filled with lukewarm, slightly colored water because the cold, clear water and the hot, colored water will mix thoroughly. This happens in your basement every time you turn on the hot-water faucet. When you turn on the faucet, the hot water flows from the tank up through the pipes and out into the sink. The hot water is pushed up and out by cold water from the cold-water supply at the bottom of the tank. The cold water flows through the pipes to the burner where it is heated. As the water gets hot, it gets lighter and the cold water forces it upward through the pipe into the tank. The coldest water in the tank, then, will be at the bottom, will flow through the coils of the heater, be heated up and

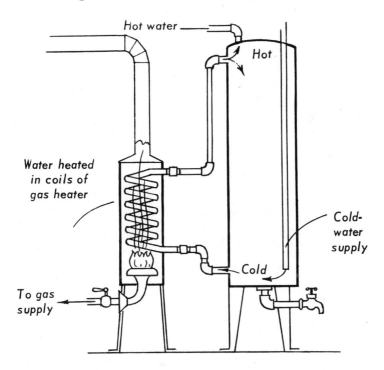

121

go to the top. New cold water will then flow through the coils until all the water in the tank is about at the same temperature waiting for you to open the hot-water faucet.

The hot-water heater in your basement may look different from the one pictured, but it works on the same principle.

The currents set up in the milk bottles and the water heater as the cold and hot water flow up and down are called "convection" currents. (Convection comes from the Latin word meaning "to carry.") The heat is carried from one place to another by currents in the water. That's the other way of getting warm . . . by convection currents.

If hot water is lighter than cold water, convection currents must be set up every time you heat water. They are, only they're hard to see. Let's make those convection currents visible by using sawdust!

EXPERIMENT 51

Materials: **Glass coffee pot**

Water

Sawdust

Source of heat

Fill the coffee pot with water and set it on the stove with only one side of the pot over the heat. When the water is boiling vigorously, add the sawdust. See how the sawdust shows the water going down on the side of the pot away from the heat and the water going up on the side of the pot nearest the heat? The sawdust will continue to go 'round and 'round.

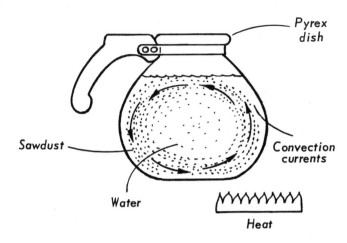

The same thing happens when the pot is sitting on the center of the heat, but then the currents bump into each other and get all mixed up.

If hot water is lighter than cold water, is hot air lighter than cold air? In a loose sense, it is. While it's hard to weigh the difference between hot and cold water, you can easily weigh the difference between hot and cold air—with a paper-bag balance.

EXPERIMENT 52

Materials: **Two paper bags the same size**

Scotch tape

String

A stick for balance

A candle

Tie a loop in the end of a piece of string and put the stick into it. Attach the string to each of the paper bags with Scotch tape and tie a bag at each end of the stick. Adjust the whole thing until it balances. Now, holding one of the paper bags lightly with your fingers, hold the lighted candle in

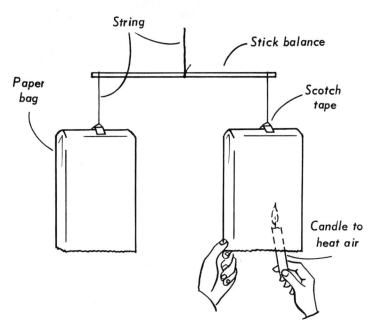

the paper bag. (Be sure you don't burn up the bag with the candle.)

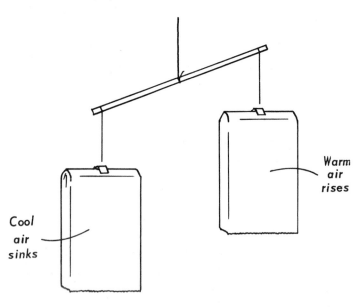

124

When you think you have held the candle in the bag long enough to have heated up the air inside, let go with your hand. Here's what happens:

The bag full of cold air sinks because the expanding hot air forces the other bag up.

Are there convection currents in air, then, as well as water? Sure.

EXPERIMENT 53

Materials: Shoe box

Short length of candle in holder

Two lamp chimneys

A smoke source such as a cigarette or burning rag

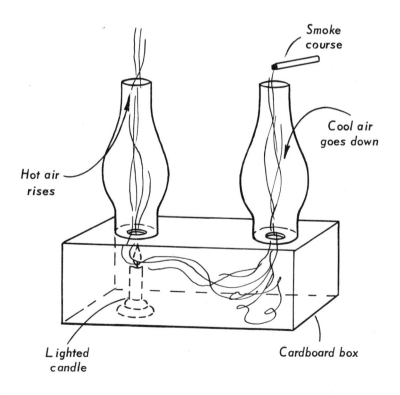

Smoke course

Cool air goes down

Hot air rises

Lighted candle

Cardboard box

In the bottom of the shoe box cut two holes smaller than the opening in the lamp chimneys. Light a candle and set the shoe box upside down over it with the candle directly below one of the holes. Set the two lamp chimneys over the holes. Hold the smoke source near the lamp chimney without the candle under it. Here's what happens to the smoke:

The air that's heated by the candle and the gases that are the result of the burning process are lighter than the air in the shoe box. The cold air in the shoe box (being pulled down more by the force of gravity) pushes the warm air up. As the cold air moves within the box, more cold air will come in through the top of the chimney. The smoke source makes the convection currents in the air visible.

See how the air moves sideways in the middle

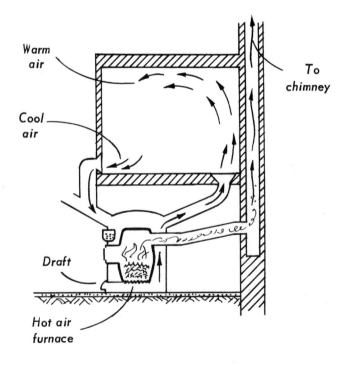

Warm air

To chimney

Cool air

Draft

Hot air furnace

of the shoe box? When the sun heats the earth (by radiant energy changed to heat energy) and the earth heats the air (by conduction), then cool air moves the warm air up (convection currents) and you call it wind!

You get hot air into the rooms of your house in the same way you get hot water—by convection currents.

The air is warmed in the furnace and pushed up by cold air coming down from the rooms upstairs. The warm air is pushed up the pipes into the room where its heat keeps you warm. The cold air is near the register at the floor and goes down to the furnace. Notice there's a draft in the furnace to supply air to the fire and a chimney for the gases to escape.

Now that we've investigated the practical aspects of convection currents, let's have fun with them.

EXPERIMENT 54

Materials: **Square of heavy writing paper about 6 inches by 6 inches**

Pencil

Scissors

Needle

Spool

Candle

Matches

Thimble

Cut a hole in the center of the heavy paper a little smaller than the thimble. Now draw a double spiral starting from the hole and going round and round it to the edge of the paper. You can draw

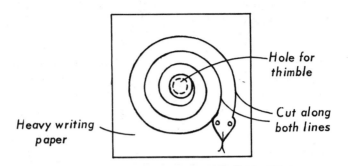

the head of a snake on the outside of the spiral if you want to. With the scissors cut along the lines as indicated.

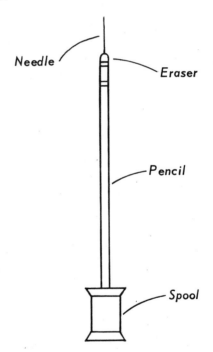

Put the eye end of the needle into the eraser of the pencil and put the point end of the pencil into the spool.

Now put the thimble in the hole in the center

of the spiral and set the whole arrangement down on the top of the needle so the thimble will rest on the needle and the spiral will twine around the pencil. Set the spool near the edge of the table and hold a candle below it. The paper snake will wind its way 'round and 'round the pencil.

The gases from the candle and the air that's heated up by the flame are pushed up by the cold air flowing up around the candle. The warm air, as it moves past the spiral, pushes against the spiral and turns it. Convection currents keep the snake going 'round and 'round.

So now you know the three ways of getting warm: by blocking radiant energy, especially from the sun, so it will change to heat energy; by conducting the heat to where you want it, or by carrying it via convection currents.

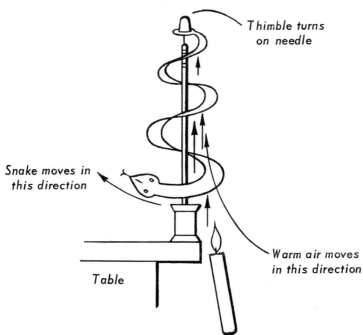

Thimble turns
on needle

Snake moves in
this direction

Warm air moves
in this direction

Table

Chapter Seven

Sound fun

YOU CAN MAKE A LION'S ROAR, a dog's bark or a jungle bird's call if you have the right-sized box.

EXPERIMENT 55

Materials: **A box (of cardboard, metal or wood)**

Pencil

String

Resin

Knife

Tie the string around the center of the pencil.

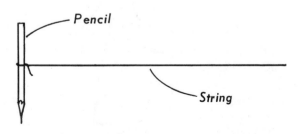

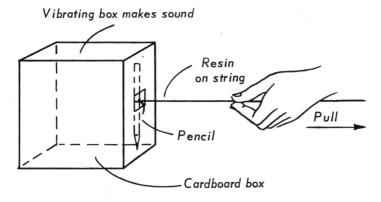

Vibrating box makes sound

Resin on string

Pull

Pencil

Cardboard box

With the knife, cut a hole in one side of the box and put the string through it with the pencil inside the box. Rub plenty of resin on the string. Hold the box with one hand and pull the string with the other.

You will hear a lion's roar, a dog's bark or a jungle bird's cry depending upon the size of the box and how you pull the string. What makes these strange sounds come from a box? Let's find out.

EXPERIMENT 56

Materials: A ruler

A table

Lay the ruler on the table and hold down one end of it with your hand. With the other hand bend the ruler and let go quickly. The ruler vibrates up and down and you hear a sound. Whenever anything vibrates hard enough and fast enough it sets up vibrations in the air which strike your ear and you hear a sound. That's how all sounds are made. Something somewhere is moving back and forth hard and fast enough to send out vibrations to your ear. What's vibrating in the box to make the animal sounds?

131

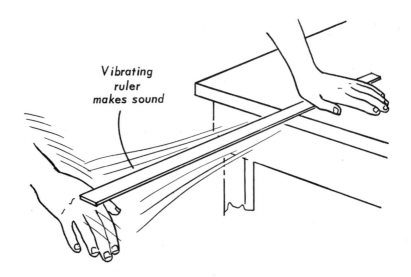

Vibrating
ruler
makes sound

When you pull on the string coated with resin you'll find that your hand sticks slightly. This makes your hand move in a series of short, fast jerks. This quick jerking motion sets the pencil to vibrating and it vibrates the whole box. A small box will vibrate fast, sending out a high-pitched sound like a jungle bird. A larger box will vibrate more slowly—a lion's roar. A medium-sized box, and a series of jerks with the hand on the string—a dog barking. Try all kinds of sizes of boxes and you'll get all kinds of eerie sounds.

You can *see* why a small box sends out a high-pitched sound and a larger box a lower-pitched sound when you watch the ruler you vibrated on the table. Move the hand holding the ruler to the table back and forth with the ruler and vibrate the other end. When a short piece of ruler is over the edge of the table you can see it vibrate fast and hear a high-pitched sound. When you move the ruler further over the edge you will see it vibrate more slowly and hear a lower-pitched sound. With practice you can play a tune by moving the ruler in and out to produce the right notes.

You can use the same ruler to make a ruler-roarer.

EXPERIMENT 57

Materials: **A ruler**

A piece of broomstick

Stout string

Drill for making holes in wood

Make a hole in one end of the ruler and the broomstick. You don't have to have a broomstick. Any strong stick of wood will work. Tie the ruler to the broomstick with a long loop of stout string. Now swing the broomstick in a circle, making the

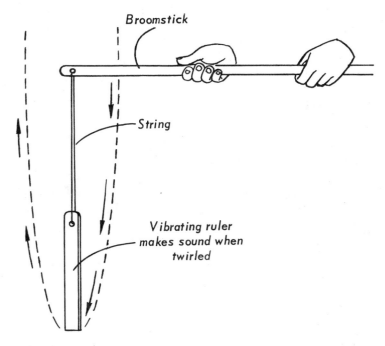

Broomstick

String

Vibrating ruler makes sound when twirled

ruler swing around in a larger circle. Here's Betsy swinging the ruler-roarer I made for her.

The ruler roars because when Betsy (or you, when you try it) swings it through the air the ruler spins very fast in such a way that it winds up the loop of string. It does this so hard and so fast that it sends out vibrations through the air which you hear as a roaring sound. This roaring stops when the string is all wound up as tight as it will go. Then the ruler spins the other way and roars as it unwinds the string. The whole process starts all over

134

again in the other direction. The ruler-roarer really roars!

Ever see someone split a wide blade of grass, hold it between their thumbs and blow a squeaky sound? You can make this same sound a lot easier with two sheets of paper.

EXPERIMENT 58

Materials: Two sheets of paper

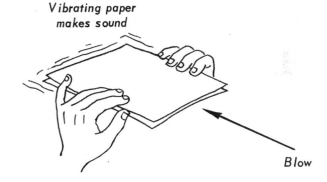

Vibrating paper makes sound

Blow

Hold the two sheets of paper so that one edge overlaps the other slightly and blow between the papers. The force of the air going between the sheets will set them to vibrating fast enough to make a squeaky, silly sound.

You can make a more beautiful sound with a table fork.

EXPERIMENT 59

Materials: Table fork

Rap the tines (the fingers) of the fork against something hard (not the furniture; you'll mar it; use an old piece of wood). The tines of the fork will vibrate, producing a musical note. It's not very loud, so you'll have to hold it up close to your ear to hear it.

Tines of fork
vibrate and
make sound

You've done tricks with air pressure, vacuums, oxidation, low-pressure areas, the center of gravity and heat. Why not sound?

EXPERIMENT 60

Materials: Table fork

Drinking glass

Table

Announce to your friends that you can carry sound in your finger tips. Rap the fork against a block of wood and touch the handle with your finger tip. With your eyes on your finger tip—and your friend's eyes too—slowly bring it to the edge of the glass. As you touch the glass, also (without your friends noticing it), touch the handle of the fork to the table. Your friends will hear a musical note that seems to come from the glass!

You know, of course, you haven't carried sound in your finger tips at all because it came from the vibrating fork. Why did the fork sound so loud when you touched the handle to the table? The sound was so weak before that you had to hold it up to your ear to hear it.

Here's the science secret: when only the tines of the table fork vibrate they set into motion only small quantities of air. That means the vibrations in the air are too weak for you to hear unless you hold the fork close to your ear. But when you touch the handle of the fork to the top of the table the vibrating fork sets the whole table vibrating. With such a large surface moving back and forth a lot more air is set into motion and the resulting louder

Touch glass
with finger

Touch table
with fork

sound is easier for you to hear. That's the reason you're able to make loud animal sounds with the box—the whole box is vibrating.

You can usually make the sound louder by adding a "sounding box" to help vibrate the air. Try the fork on anything that's handy like an empty coffee can.

EXPERIMENT 61

Materials: Table fork

Empty coffee can

Rap the fork and touch the handle of it to the edge of the coffee can. You'll hear a loud pleasant sound. Does the coffee can have to be empty? Yes. Why? Because for it to work as a sounding box and increase the volume of the sound it must be able to vibrate as fast as the fork. The sounding box, whatever it is made of, can't be too heavy or it will be hard to set it moving back and forth. The coffee in the can will prevent the can from vibrating very much. The idea is to get the air around the can moving with as much force as possible. The easier it is for the can to vibrate, the better.

Vibrating coffee can Increases volume of sound

Table fork vibrating

EXPERIMENT 62

Materials: A table fork

A drinking glass

Rap the fork and touch the handle to the rim of the drinking glass. You'll hear a fairly loud, pleasant note. If you've been using the same fork all along, try using other forks of different lengths and shapes.

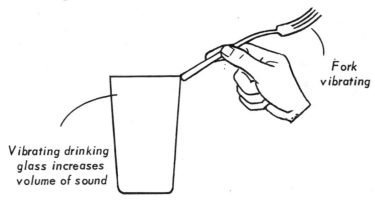

Fork vibrating

Vibrating drinking glass increases volume of sound

If you flick the rim of the drinking glass with your finger, the whole glass will vibrate and you'll hear a musical note, the pitch of which will be determined by the size of the glass and how fast it can vibrate. If you happen to have a violin bow around the house, you can really get music out of an empty glass.

EXPERIMENT 63

Materials: Empty drinking glass

Violin bow

Resin

(If you don't happen to have a violin bow around the house you can still do this. I'll tell you how later on)

Joan Begonia

Hold the glass with one hand and stroke the violin bow across the rim with the other. Be sure to have plenty of resin on the bow. You'll hear a note as long as you keep moving the bow. Willy could hardly believe his ears when he saw me do it.

The resin on the bow vibrates the glass in the same way as the resin on the string vibrated the animal sound boxes. Try various sizes of glasses for various notes.

If you don't have a violin bow handy you can make a substitute like this: cut a strip of cotton cloth about an inch wide and two feet long. Rub resin thoroughly over one side of it. Hold one end in each hand and have someone hold the glass. Pull the cloth "bow" along the rim of the glass as I did the violin bow. Use plenty of resin and it will work fine.

If you like to make things with tools and want

140

to see sand dance to the vibrations of a sound, try building this.

EXPERIMENT 64

Materials: **Piece of glass**

Cork split into halves

Fine sand

Violin bow

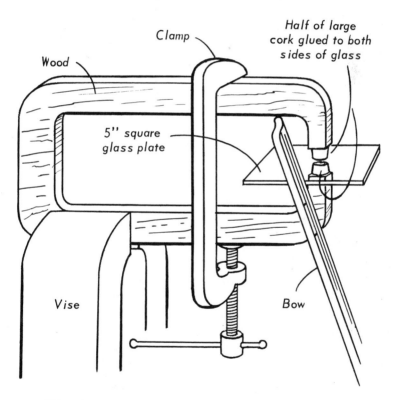

The dimensions aren't too important as long as you clamp the glass plate securely in the middle with the halves of the cork and still allow the glass to vibrate. Sprinkle fine sand evenly over the glass plate and bow the edge with a violin bow at various places. Try bowing with one hand and holding the edge of the glass plate with the two fingers of the other hand. You'll see figures like these:

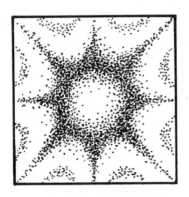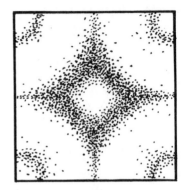

As the plate vibrates it makes the sand hop up and down. Wherever the plate is vibrating most it rolls the sand away. The sand collects in those places where the plate is vibrating least. The patterns formed show you how the glass is vibrating.

So far the sound produced by all the things you've set into vibration have reached your ear by traveling through the air. There must be something for sound waves to travel through, but it doesn't have to be air. It can be string!

EXPERIMENT 65

Materials: A spoon

A length of string

Cut the string to the proper length so that you can hold one end of it in each of your ears with your finger tips. Balance the spoon in the loop formed when you lean over. Now swing the spoon against a chair or table leg and will you be surprised! Willy

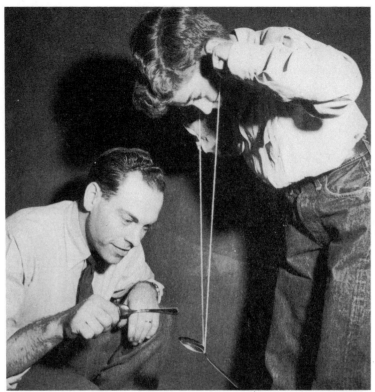

Parade

was when he heard what went up the string to his ears.

Because it was easier for Willy, I rapped the spoon balanced on the string instead of having Willy rap it against the table leg. Aren't you surprised at what you hear coming up the string? It depends on the size and shape of the spoon, of course, but the one Willy and I used sounded exactly like the chimes in a church steeple. Whatever your spoon sounds like, it will ring plenty loud because the vibrations of the spoon, instead of having to travel through the air, go right up the string which ends in your ears.

You can hear some amazingly beautiful sounds

all at the same time, perhaps in harmony, like this:

EXPERIMENT 66

Materials: String

        A knife

        A fork

        A spoon

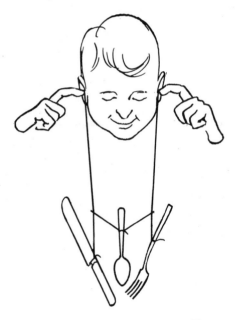

Attach whatever you want to listen to to the middle of the string.

What you hear depends on what you vibrate.

What you hear in the tin can in the next experiment depends on what your friends say into another tin can in the next room!

EXPERIMENT 67

Materials: Two tin cans

        A long length of cotton string

Punch a small hole in the exact center of the bottom of each tin can. Thread one end of the string through the bottom of one of the cans and out through the top. Tie a knot bulky enough to prevent the string from being pulled back out through the hole.

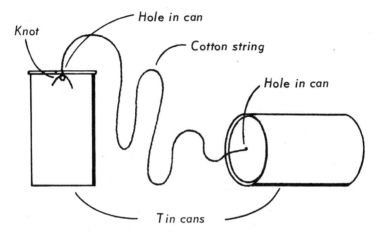

Thread the other end of the string through the hole in the other can.

Have a friend take the can with the knot in it into the other room, keeping the string straight. When he is as far away as he can get and still keep the string straight, pull the string through the hole in your can, cut if off and tie a knot in the end. When both of you hold your tin cans up to your mouths or ears (depending on who's talking and who's listening), and keep the string between the cans fairly tight, you'll be able to talk back and forth because you've made a tin-can telephone. Betsy and Willy installed a private line of their own.

Did you notice I said the string between the tin cans had to be kept in a straight line? If you try

to turn a corner and let the string touch the edge of a door or some other rigid object, the vibrations traveling down the string will be stopped. You'll be "temporarily disconnected" until you and your friend get straightened out. However, you can turn a corner with your string telephone line. On one end of a short piece of string tie a loop around the "telephone line" string at the place where you want it to go around the corner. Then tie the other end of the short piece of string to anything convenient and in such a way that the telephone line is held away from the corner by the short piece of string. The telephone line can now vibrate freely right around the corner and even up the stairs if you want it to!

Scientists with accurate and delicate instruments have timed the speed at which sound waves travel through various materials. Have you ever listened to sound under water? Sound travels a lot faster in water than it does in air. Have you ever put your ear to a railroad track and heard the train coming long before you could see it? (Look both ways before you try this; the track is no place for your ear to be with a train bearing down on you!) Have a friend tap the track with a stone. You'll be amazed at how far and how fast the sound travels through the rails. If there is nothing for the sound waves to travel through, there is no sound. In a vacuum, sound just isn't.

Most of the time, though, the sound waves travel to your ear through the air. Scientists have clocked the speed of sound in air at approximately 1100 feet per second. With this one simple fact, a watch with a second hand on it, and the knowledge of how to divide by five, you can tell how far away the next bolt of lightning is.

EXPERIMENT 68

Materials: **A watch with a second hand**

Knowledge of how to divide by five

A bolt of lightning

A clap of thunder

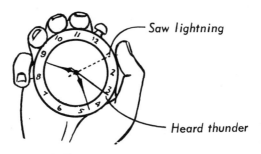

The moment you see the lightning flash note the position of the second hand on the watch. Keep looking at it until you hear the crash of thunder. Note how many seconds have elapsed. Let's say it was 10 seconds from the time you saw the lightning until you heard the thunder.

There are 5280 feet in a mile and sound travels approximately 1100 feet per second through the air. 5280 divided by 1100 is roughly 5. Therefore sound waves travel about a mile in 5 seconds. You heard the thunder 10 seconds after you saw the lightning. 10 divided by 5 is 2. Therefore the lighting was about 2 miles away.

The speed of the sound that comes from an orchestra isn't nearly so important as the kind of sounds the musicians make with their instruments. Different kinds of sounds come from different kinds of instruments. With rubber bands, bottles, a vacuum cleaner and other things found around the house, you can make your own musical instruments.

Chapter Eight

The bottle, pin and soda-straw philharmonic

I'D BETTER WARN YOU right now that the instruments you make for your bottle, pin and soda-straw philharmonic orchestra won't make quite the same sounds as those in a real orchestra. But all of them will produce sounds in the same way the real instruments do. To produce a musical sound you are going to have to make something vibrate, and vibrate fast and loud enough to hear it. What kind of a musical instrument can you make with a metal baking dish and rubber bands?

EXPERIMENT 69

Materials: A baking dish

Rubber bands of various sizes

Stretch the rubber bands around the baking dish. Adjust the tension of each one to a different pitch and pluck them. The rubber bands vibrate

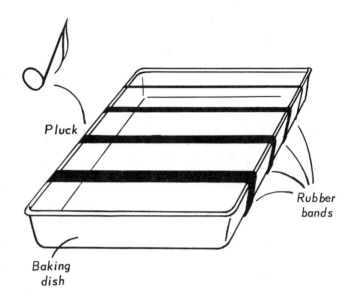

Pluck

Rubber bands

Baking dish

and the baking dish acts as a sounding box to increase the volume of the sound.

Whether you can play the scale, a tune or chords depends on how many rubber bands you use, their size and how tight you stretch them. If you haven't guessed what instruments you've just made a model of, here they are. Find the vibrating strings and the sounding box.

United Press

SCIENCE SECRETS ∿∿∿∿∿∿∿∿∿∿∿∿∿

When you play the harp you vibrate its strings by plucking. When you play the piano you vibrate its strings by hitting each one of them with a little hammer when you press down on the key. The length of each string in both cases determines the pitch of the note you hear.

You play different notes on other instruments by changing the length of the string that vibrates.

EXPERIMENT 70

Materials: **A board**

Thin steel wire

Clothespins

A nail

A weight

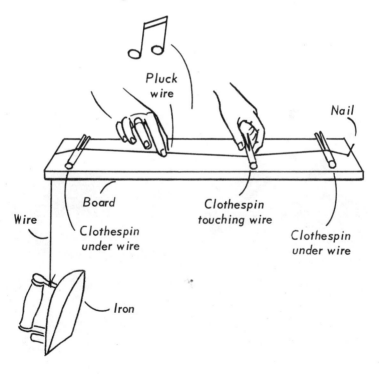

Nail

Board

Wire

Clothespin under wire

Clothespin touching wire

Clothespin under wire

Iron

Put the materials together on top of a table, letting the weight hang over the edge.

When you pluck the string with your finger, the pitch of the note you'll hear depends on several things—the thickness of the wire, how heavy the weight is and where you hold the clothespin on top of the wire. All these things determine how fast the wire can vibrate. The board vibrates too, of course, increasing the volume of the sound. By moving the clothespin back and forth as you pluck the string, you'll hear different notes. The instruments in an orchestra that work in the same way have more than one string, but each one is "fingered" to shorten or lengthen the vibrating part of each string. What instruments am I talking about?

Each member of the violin family is usually played with a bow to vibrate the strings while the guitar and ukelele and other instruments like them are played with a pick or the fingers to vibrate the strings. All of them are "fingered" to change the lengths of the vibrating strings.

United Press

152

You can make delicate, charming music with common straight pins.

EXPERIMENT 71

Materials: **Common straight pins**

A board (or, better yet, a wooden cigar box)

A piece of dowel or a pencil

Hammer

Pliers

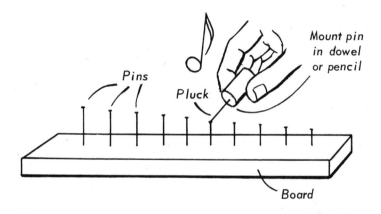

Into the light board or the wooden cigar box, drive the pins in a straight line. You'll probably have to cut off some of the pins with the pliers, else you'll bend them when you try to drive them into the wood. Notice how short the pins get toward the right side of the line.

Mount another pin in a dowel or the eraser end of a pencil and use it to pluck the pins in the board. The notes you hear will depend on how much of each pin is free to vibrate. The longer pins are your low notes and the shorter pins your higher notes. Tune each pin to the scale by pounding it further into the wood if it's too low and pulling it out slightly with the pliers if it's too high. The wooden cigar box will produce better music because it's a better sounding box than a plain board. You aren't very likely to find an instrument in a symphony orchestra that works on the principle of vibrating pins, but you've heard the music of instruments that do many times.

The music box plays a tune because little metal pegs on the revolving drum pluck the right metal "pins." You play a tune on a mouth organ when you blow or draw in the holes and vibrate the little "pins" at the back. You play a tune on an accordion when you pump air from the bellows into similar holes and pins. What tune you play depends upon which keys you press, because the keys open the holes and let the air vibrate the pins.

United Press

When you get to the bottom of an ice-cream soda you sometimes make a sound with the straw. The sound you made then isn't nearly as pleasant as the sound you can make now with a soda straw . . . and a pair of scissors.

EXPERIMENT 72

Materials: Soda straw

Scissors

Pinch one end of the soda straw flat for about ¾ of an inch from the end. Next cut the corners

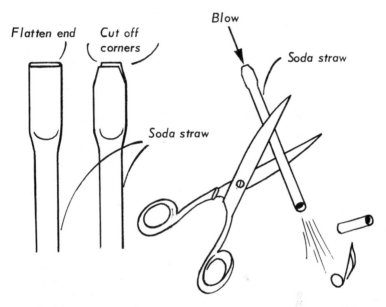

of the flat end off diagonally with the scissors. Now blow gently through the "reeds" you've made.

It takes a little practice to find out how hard to blow and how to adjust the "reed" with your lips to vibrate it. Don't blow too hard. Wait until you hear the soft music that comes out of the straw!

What's vibrating? Yes, it's true the little "reeds" are vibrating but they're really not making the musical notes. When you blow into the straw, the reeds moving back and forth open and close letting more and then less air into the straw. The column of air inside the straw thus has more and then less pressure at one end of it as it vibrates back and forth. This vibrating column of air is what makes the sound! If you find that hard to believe, consider this: when you play a tune on your pin music box, the shorter the pin, the higher the note. Right? The vibrating reeds at the end of your musical soda straw won't change in size when you cut short pieces off the other end with the scissors, will they? Certainly not. Yet the notes you play on the soda straw go up and up as you cut off the end! If you try for a real high note with the scissors . . . remember your nose! The vibrating *air column* is getting shorter and shorter as you cut off the end of the straw. The notes you play are pitched according to the length of the air column vibrating in the straw.

Almost every orchestra has a soda-straw type of instrument in it.

Which of the instruments from the "woodwind" family is most like your soda straw? The oboe and the bassoon, because both have two reeds that vibrate. The saxophones and clarinets have only one.

A column of air that vibrates fast and hard enough to make a sound is used in other kinds of instruments too. Here's one.

EXPERIMENT 73

Materials: A large funnel

Purse your lips together tightly while you hold the small end of the funnel against them and blow through the funnel. When you get the tension of your lips just right you'll blow a note. Your lips are vibrating the air column inside the funnel the same way the reeds did in your soda-straw "oboe."

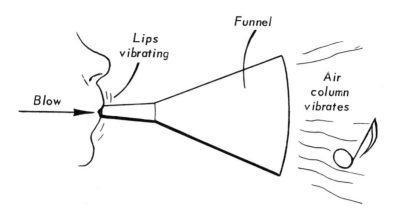

Funnel

Lips
vibrating

Blow

Air
column
vibrates

If you change the tension of your lips you may be able to blow a different note. If you do, you've changed the speed of the vibrating air column. Because the length of the funnel is fixed, the number of notes you can blow by changing the tension of your lips is limited. To blow a lot of different notes you'll have to not only change the tension of your lips but also the length of the air column. You can't very well cut off the end of the funnel as you did the soda straw. So if you want to play more notes than are possible with your funnel "bugle" you'd better get a real instrument with valves made to change the length of the air column with ease. You have a choice of several—trumpet, cornet, tuba, etc.

If you could slide the tube in which the column of air is vibrating and, that way, make the air column shorter or longer, you wouldn't need valves. Try it this way.

EXPERIMENT 74

Materials: Pop bottle

Glass tube

Water

157

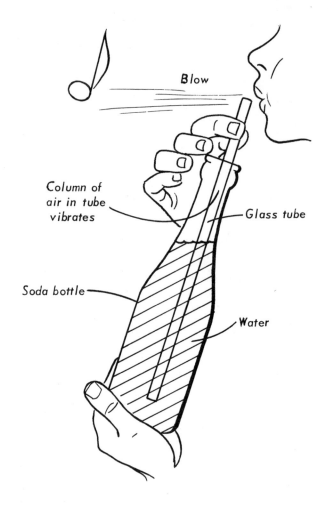

Hold the bottle in one hand and the end of the glass tube in the other. Adjust the angle of the opening at the end of the tube until you can blow a note across it. As you blow, move the bottle up and down. You'll hear various notes as you change the length of the column of air vibrating in the tube. You've probably figured out that it's the trombone which works like that.

When you played your pop-bottle "trombone" you made music all right, but how? No reeds! Blow another note on your "trombone." Then take out the glass tube, dump the water out of the bottle and blow across its mouth like you did the glass tube.

A pleasant note comes out of the bottle. It's a lot lower than any of those you could play on the "trombone." Doesn't that suggest what's vibrating? The air in the bottle (and in that part of the glass tube above the water in your pop-bottle "trombone") is vibrating, all right. Now, why?

Way back in Chapter I you had a friend try to blow up a balloon inside of a bottle. He didn't do very well because he couldn't compress the air in the bottle very much. When you blow across the top of the bottle you compress the air inside of the bottle too. The air pressure inside the bottle increases (like it did when the balloon expanded inside of it) until the air is under enough pressure to push its way back out of the bottle. The pressure in the bottle drops, but, because you're still blowing,

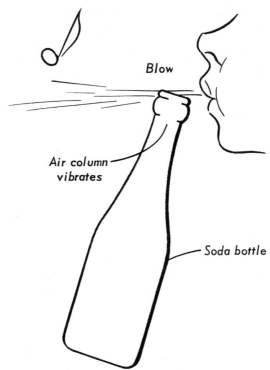

Blow

Air column
vibrates

Soda bottle

it builds right back up again. This happens fast and hard enough to . . . you know what. The larger the bottle, the longer it will take the air pressure to build up, the slower the vibrations of the air in the bottle . . . and the lower the note you'll blow.

You'll soon be all blown out if you keep this up. Get out the vacuum cleaner, put the hose attachment in the *blower* end and turn on the motor. Try the bottle again. In spite of the increase in the amount of air going across the mouth, the same note comes out. Try the same thing with a milk bottle. If you let your imagination go when you hear what comes out of the milk bottle, you'll be floatin' down the Mississippi. There's a steamboat whistle in a milk bottle!

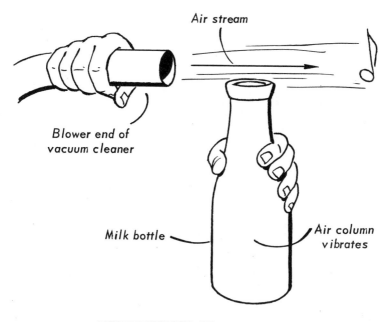

Air stream

Blower end of
vacuum cleaner

Milk bottle

Air column
vibrates

EXPERIMENT 75

Materials: **Bottles of various sizes**

          Water

          Vacuum cleaner

A musical instrument on which you can play melodies with the blower end of a vacuum cleaner is the next step, of course. Round up various sizes of bottles, line them up according to size and tune them by adding water to those that are a little too low in pitch.

Don't forget you're putting together musical instruments found in an orchestra. What instruments have you just made? (Well, you've used the same principles, anyway.)

You play a pipe organ by pressing keys to send air "across" various sizes of "bottles" or pipes. You play a piccolo or a flute by holding your fingers over

Blower end of vacuum cleaner

Various sized bottles

Air columns vibrate

Water

various holes to make one "bottle" into "bottles" of various lengths.

When you have had enough vacuum-cleaner organ music, don't put the bottles back. You can put the vacuum cleaner away if you want to, though. Get a table knife on your way back.

EXPERIMENT 76

Materials: Bottles of various sizes

Table knife

Water

With the handle of the dinner knife, gently tap the bottles you used to make the organ. Even though you haven't changed a single bottle, you won't get the same notes as before. This time it's the *bottle itself* that vibrates, not the column of air inside of it.

Tune the bottles with the water again and you'll find another difference. The more water you added before, the shorter the air column and the higher the note. Now when you add water as you tap the bottle, the more water, the lower the note! The more there is to whatever is vibrating, the slower it can go. More water means slower vibrating and a lower note. With the bottles tuned to the scale, pick out a tune. What are you playing in an orchestra?

The man who tunes a xylophone cuts off each cross piece to the proper length. The man who tunes the chimes does the same thing to each metal tube.

So far you've made every type of instrument in an orchestra except one: the drums.

EXPERIMENT 77

Materials: **Empty coffee can**

Large balloon

String

Soda straws

Scissors

Nail

Hammer

Punch a hole in the side of the coffee can with the nail and the hammer. Cut a large rubber balloon in half and stretch it over the top of the coffee can. Tie the balloon in place with the string (a rubber band may work better). You can beat out a neat rhythm with the two soda straws as drumsticks.

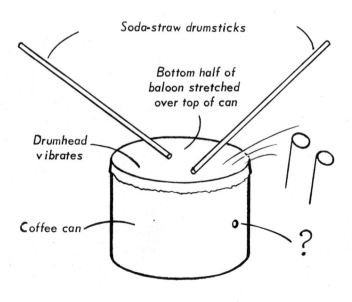

Soda-straw drumsticks

Bottom half of
baloon stretched
over top of can

Drumhead
vibrates

Coffee can

A drum is so simple to make there is no mystery about how you can make the sound on it . . . but what's the hole in the side for?

First, what's vibrating? The rubber balloon "drumhead" is vibrating. The tighter you stretch it, the higher the note from the drum. That's because the drumhead vibrates faster. Without the hole in the side of your drum what would happen to the air inside when the drumhead started down as it vibrates? The air would be compressed, wouldn't it? The drumhead won't vibrate as well with a "cushion" of air under it. You reduce the cushioning effect of the air by putting a hole in the side of the can for the air to go in and out as the drumhead goes up and down. Next time you're around an orchestra, look for that hole in the drum.

For that matter, look at all the instruments in the orchestra. They'll be especially interesting to you because you've made one that works like every instrument there is!

United Press

Chapter Nine

The case of the
mysterious magnet

IF A MAGNET is a mysterious piece of metal to you,
don't worry, it's mysterious to everybody else too.
But scientists are investigating how a magnet
works and they've got a good "theory." (A scientific
theory is an idea that fits all known facts but has to
be proven still further before it can be accepted as
a "law.") Once you uncover the key evidence, the case
of the mysterious magnet isn't so mysterious after
all. Here's some of the evidence scientists have un-
covered so far to prove their case.

EXPERIMENT 78

Materials: **A magnet**

Iron filings or other bits of iron or steel

Piece of paper

Any magnet will do. You can buy iron filings
from a scientific supply house, get them from a ma-

chine shop or make your own with a file and a piece of soft iron. You don't need them, really, for this experiment, but you'll certainly want them later on.

Spread the paper on the table and sprinkle iron filings or other bits of iron or steel on it. You could use tacks, pins or paper clips. The paper keeps the iron filings from dirtying the table. Bring the magnet close to the iron and you'll see the magnet attract bits of iron to it.

A simple experiment? Sure, but a very important one. Try picking up bits of aluminum, glass, sand or paper. The magnet ignores them completely. Long ago men noticed this force that "lodestone" (as

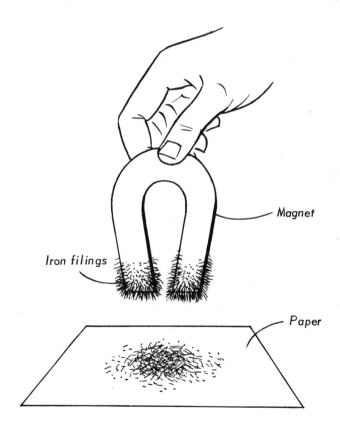

Magnet

Iron filings

Paper

early magnets were called) could exert on iron. They duly noted this in their notebooks and time went on.

Eventually, one of these scientific "detectives" wondered what would happen when, instead of bringing a magnet and a piece of iron together, you brought two magnets together. Well, let's see.

EXPERIMENT 79

Materials: Two magnets

Adhesive or friction tape

You can use either horseshoe or bar magnets. If you have bar magnets and the ends are marked with "N" and "S," wrap a layer of tape around the "N" end of one and the "S" end of the other about a half an inch from the end. If there are no marks, wrap tape around one end of each and do the experiment below. If it turns out that the ends are marked as they are in the drawings, fine. If not, take the tape off the end of *one* magnet and wrap it around the other end.

If you have horseshoe magnets, treat them as if they were a bar magnet bent into the shape of a horseshoe, because that's all they really are.

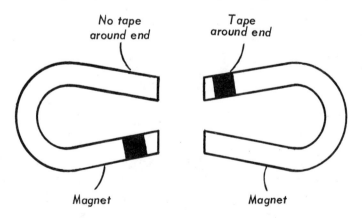

No tape around end   Tape around end

Magnet   Magnet

Magnets
come together

Magnets
go apart

Wrap one end of each magnet and try the experiment, changing the tape from one end to the other if it doesn't correspond to the drawings. Here's what happens when you get the right ends of the magnets marked with tape.

When you bring the ends of the magnets near each other and the taped end is opposite a bare end, the magnets will move toward each other and touch or attract. When two taped ends are opposite, the magnets will move away from each other or repel. Neither end of the magnet did this with the bits of iron. Both ends attracted the iron filings. There's a clue that deepens the mystery. There seems to be more to these magnets than a simple attraction for iron and steel (and a few other rare metals). If you got some iron filings before, here's where you can use them like a real detective uses fingerprint dust.

EXPERIMENT 80

Materials: Two magnets

          A pane of glass or very smooth, stiff paper

          Iron filings

On a table lay the magnets close together but not touching, with a taped end opposite a bare end. Place the pane of glass over them and sprinkle the iron filings on the glass over the ends of the magnets.

Glass plate over magnets

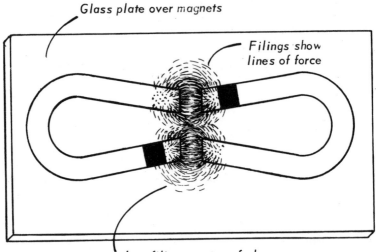

Filings show
lines of force

Iron filings on top of glass

The force of the magnets goes right through the glass or paper to attract the iron filings and they make visible the lines of force of the magnets. See how the lines of force go straight across between the ends and curve from one to the other at the sides?

Glass plate over magnets

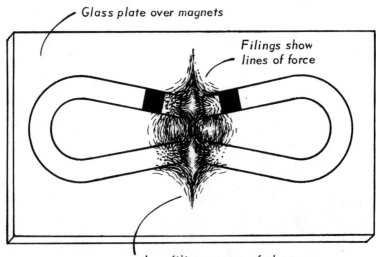

Filings show
lines of force

Iron filings on top of glass

You are looking at the "fingerprints" of the lines of force that are trying to pull the magnets together.

Now pick up the glass, dump the filings onto a piece of paper and turn *one* of the magnets upside down, making sure the ends are close together but not touching. Replace the glass and sprinkle on the iron filings.

This time the iron filing "fingerprints" are dif-

Ben and Sid Ross

ferent! Remember that in this position the magnets tried to move away or repel each other. No longer are there straight lines of force from one end to the other. This time the lines of force curve away from the ends almost as though the opposing ends didn't like each other. I've got an especially powerful horseshoe magnet in my home laboratory. You can see, on page 171, what happened when I covered the ends with glass, put Willy's hand over the glass and sprinkled plenty of iron filings on his hand.

Willy couldn't feel the force of the magnet on his hand, but he could feel the force of the magnet pulling the iron filings down.

You know from your last two clues that the ends of a magnet are different as far as attracting and repelling are concerned. Maybe your magnets are already marked with an "N" or an "S," or perhaps you already know from your experience in previous magnetic "cases" that one end of a magnet is called the "north pole" and the other the "south pole." When the north and the south poles of two magnets come near each other they attract. When either two north poles or two south poles come together they repel. Another way of saying it is, "Unlike poles attract; like poles repel." When you had a marked pole on your magnet opposite an unmarked one you must have had a north and a south pole opposite each other on each side because the magnets attracted each other. When you had the two marked ends together you must have had two north poles or two south poles opposite each other because the magnets repelled each other. But which end is which? Are the marked ends two north poles or two south poles? To find out you will have to send the evidence to the laboratory for analysis and make a new magnet.

EXPERIMENT 81

Materials: **Magnet**

Iron filings

Sewing needle

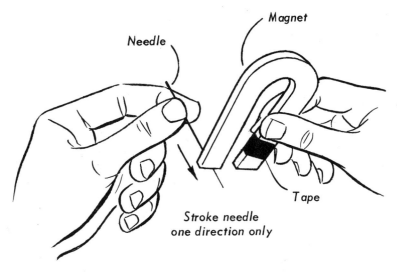

Magnet

Needle

Tape

Stroke needle
one direction only

Stroke one end of the needle with one end of the magnet. Stroke in *one direction only;* and with *one end of the magnet only.* Do this a couple dozen times and then put the needle into the iron filings. If it doesn't pick up the filings, repeat the stroking again with the *same end of the needle* and the *same end of the magnet.* When you can pick up iron filings with the needle you've made a new magnet out of the needle. Now to put it to use in unraveling this puzzling case.

EXPERIMENT 82

Materials: **Magnet**

Magnetized needle

Cork

Glass of water

Knife

Slice one end of the cork off with the knife until the cork will float flat on the water in the glass. Cut a slit across the top of the middle of the cork deep enough to hold the needle. Press the needle into the slit. Now float the cork and needle in the glass. You've got a floating magnet, free to turn in any direction on the water. The point of the needle will be either a north or south pole, depending on which end of the magnet you rubbed it with. Bring one end of the magnet near the outside of the glass. You'll see the needle turn around to this position:

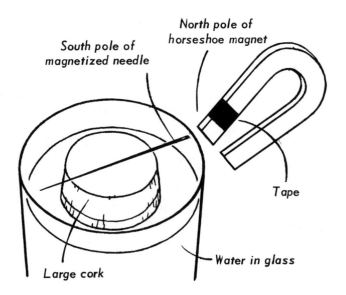

Don't get too close to the needle with the magnet; just close enough to make the needle move. Without changing the direction that the needle points, bring the other end of the magnet near it. The needle will swing around until the other end is near the magnet. This is what you'd expect when you bring unlike and like poles together. Did you know you've just made a magnetic compass?

EXPERIMENT 83

Materials: The floating compass you just made

You see, the earth is a magnet with lines of force, too. You've heard of the north and south magnetic poles; they're the ends of the magnet we live on.

When a magnet is free to turn, it acts the same

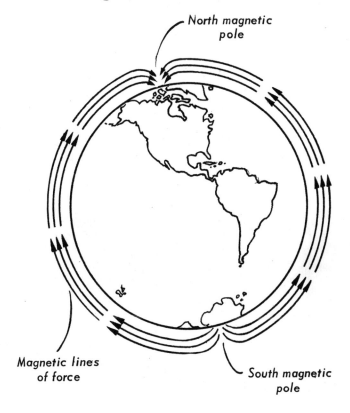

North magnetic
pole

Magnetic lines
of force

South magnetic
pole

way in the earth's magnetic lines of force as the needle did in the lines of magnetic force you brought close to it. Remove all iron and steel from near the needle and it swings around so one end of it points to the north magnetic pole of the earth. The end that does that is called the "north" or "north seeking" end. The other end points to the south and is called the "south" or "south seeking" end. With these simple pieces of laboratory apparatus you can now not only tell in which direction the north magnetic pole is, but you can also tell which of the ends of your magnet is north. You're getting pretty close to solving the case of the mysterious magnet!

EXPERIMENT 84

Materials: Sewing-needle compass

Magnet

Allow the needle of your homemade compass to swing until one end is pointing north. This is the

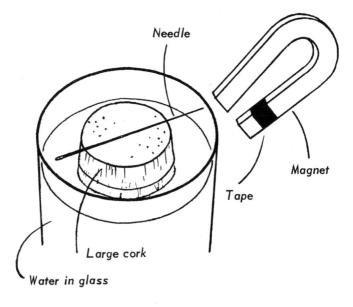

Needle

Magnet

Tape

Large cork

Water in glass

north pole of the magnetized needle. Now, when you bring one end of the marked magnet near the needle, and the needle turns toward it, you know that that end of the magnet is the south pole (seems strange but the kind of magnetism at the magnetic north pole of the earth must actually be a south pole too if the north end of the compass actually points to it!). If the north end of the needle turns away from the end of the magnet it must be a north pole because "like poles repel." Whether it's the taped end or untaped end that attracts the north pole of the sewing needle compass will depend on which end you taped before. Find the ends of all your magnets that attract the south end of the compass, put tape on those ends and mark an "N" on the tape.

Put tape on the other end and mark with an "S." If you want to, you can repeat the experiment with the pane of glass and iron filings.

The case of the mysterious magnet is almost solved. One more question to clear up: why was the needle *not* a magnet *before* you stroked it and definitely a magnet *after* you stroked it with another magnet? Here's the case presented by the scientists.

The needle is made up of very, very small particles of steel, each of which is a very, very small magnet. When the needle was made, the magnetized particle within it looked like this:

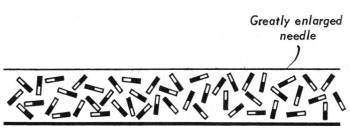

Greatly enlarged needle

Not magnetized

Because the poles of the particles are pointing every which way they sort of counteract each other and no magnetism can be detected. If you could bring a magnet near the little particles and get them to move, their north poles would turn toward the south poles of the magnet. That's what you did when you stroked the needle with the magnet; you lined up the poles of the particles like this:

Magnetic

Each time you stroked the needle with the magnet you lined up more of the particles. Notice that at one end of the needle, the north poles of the particles are facing out. This end of the needle is the north end of the magnet. The particles of your other magnets are lined up in a similar way. When an outside force of some kind throws the particles out of line and mixes them up again the magnetic effect disappears. Heat will do this; so will pounding or repeated dropping of the magnet.

If the scientists are correct in their theory, you should be able to cut a magnet in half any place and have two magnets instead of one. Pretend to cut the lined-up particles in the drawing and you'll see that no matter where you cut it, the north poles will point one way and the south poles the other. Why not test the theory?

EXPERIMENT 85

Materials: Magnetized needle

Pliers or wire cutters

178

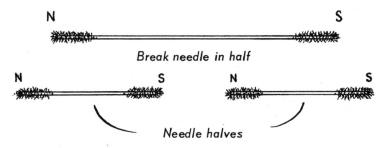

N   S

Break needle in half

N   S   N   S

Needle halves

You'd better keep the compass just as it is for future use and magnetize another needle by stroking it with a magnet. Break or cut the needle in two with the pliers or cutters. Test the ends of the two new pieces by dipping them in iron filings. Each piece of the needle is a magnet with north and south poles.

It's now time to sum up the evidence of the case: iron and steel (and a few other rarer metals) are attracted to either end of a magnet. This is not true when the iron or steel is another magnet. Then the two magnets will attract each other when the opposing poles are "N" and "S" and repel each other when the opposing poles are "N" and "N" or "S" and "S," for unlike poles attract and like poles repel. You can make a magnet by stroking a piece of iron or steel with another magnet because you line up most of the particles of the iron or steel so that their poles face in one direction. Now the case of the mysterious magnet is solved at last, at least for all practical purposes. There are still deeper mysteries to be solved and scientists are hard at work on them. You, however, are ready for fun . . . fun with magnets that may fool your friends!

EXPERIMENT 86

Materials: **Strong magnet**

Aluminum pan

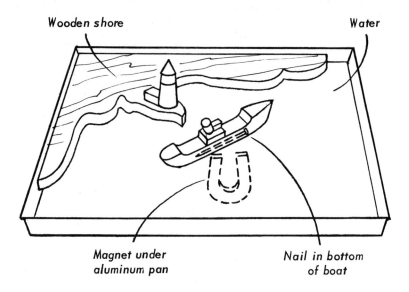

Wooden shore   Water

Magnet under   Nail in bottom
aluminum pan   of boat

Nail

Wood for various parts of the mystery ship

In an aluminum pan build an ocean like that shown. The dimensions of the shore and the boat will be dictated by the size of the pan. Fix a nail in the bottom of the boat, fill the pan with enough water to float it and move the boat over the high seas with the magnet under the pan. Be sure to use only aluminum, wood, water, or other nonmagnetic materials in the construction of the shore. The boat will cruise after the magnet because of the iron nail in its keel.

EXPERIMENT 87

Materials: Magnet

                Two books

                Iron washers

While your "passengers" are on their magnetic

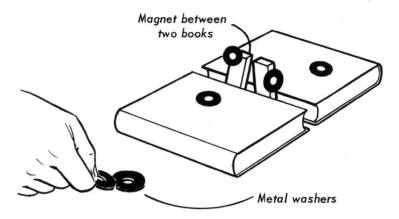

Magnet between two books

Metal washers

cruise, perhaps they'd like to play magnetic tiddly-winks.

Set the magnets up between two books and use the washers as tiddly-winks. You can decide on your own scoring rules. Perhaps something like this: 7 points for a washer flat on the upper end of the magnet, 3 for a washer on a magnet and not touching a book, 1 for a washer touching a magnet and a book, no score unless a washer actually touches the magnet. Take turns and see who gets the highest score. Then see if the winner is equally good at this:

EXPERIMENT 88

Materials: **Large-mouthed bottle**

Iron washers

Identical magnets

Get a large bottle with the mouth larger than the diameter of the washer. Toss the washers in the bottle and, with a magnet, get each washer to a different side of the bottle. On a starting signal each player must use his magnet to get his washer out of the neck of the bottle.

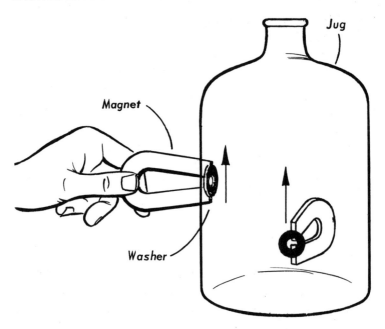

First one out gets to try his hand at the race of the magnetic jumping beans.

EXPERIMENT 89

Materials: **Gelatine capsules**

Steel ball bearings

Identical magnets

Identical cardboard boxes

Get the gelatin capsules from a drug store.

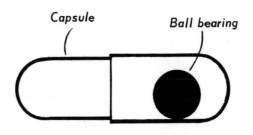

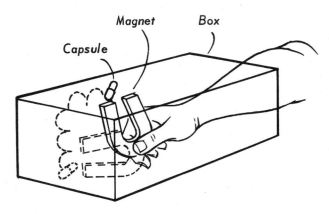

Capsule Magnet Box

They're used to put medical powders or liquids in, but you're going to put in a steel ball instead.

Cut the back ends out of the identical boxes. Each player places his capsule on the table in front of his box and, with the magnet held inside the box, tries, at the starting signal, to get his capsule up the end of the box and along the top. The player that can do this first and present his capsule on the magnet wins. The capsule turns end over end like a jumping bean as the magnet pulls the ball bearing along.

You made magnets out of needles by stroking them with another magnet. Now you're going to make magnets another way—by using, of all things, electricity!

Chapter Ten

Electromagnetic magic

ONE DAY when Betsy and Willy came over to the laboratory in the back of my house I asked Betsy to tap a piece of cardboard with black pepperlike specks on it and Willy to say the magic word, "Electromagnetism." Imagine their surprise when they saw the black specks form a question mark!

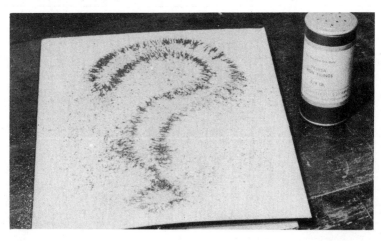

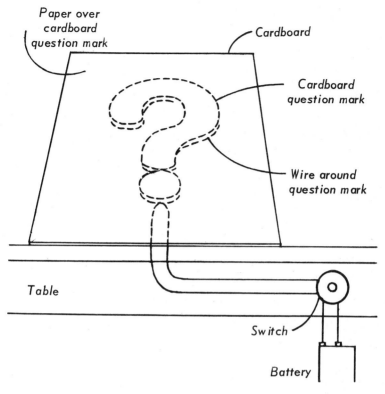

Paper over cardboard question mark

Cardboard

Cardboard question mark

Wire around question mark

Table

Switch

Battery

Of course, they wanted to know my science secret. Here's how you can make one too.

EXPERIMENT 90

Materials: **Several sheets of cardboard**

Bell wire

Iron filings

Door-bell dry cell

Door-bell pushbutton

Scotch tape

Cut a question mark out of a sheet of thick cardboard and tape it to another sheet. Tape a wire around the edge of the question mark, run it to a hidden pushbutton (any kind of switch will work), and then to the dry cell. Now cover the first sheet of cardboard with the question mark on it with a second sheet.

When you sprinkle iron filings on the top cardboard, turn on the electric current and tap the top cardboard, the filings will be attracted to the wire and form a question mark. You may need more than one dry cell.

Why do the filings move to the wire? Because magnetism is produced when an electric current goes through a wire! That's what "electromagnetism" means and that's why I had Willy say the "magic" word, "Electromagnetism."

"Fingerprint" the magnetic lines of force around a wire carrying a current as you did in the case of the mysterious magnet.

EXPERIMENT 91

Materials: **Bell wire**

Sheet of cardboard

Dry cell

Switch

Iron filings

Punch a hole through the center of the cardboard, run a wire through it and connect it through the switch to the dry cell. Holding the cardboard level, sprinkle iron filings around the wire. Turn on the current and tap the cardboard. The iron filings will outline the circular magnetic field around the wire.

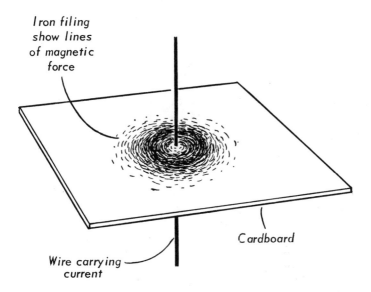

Iron filing
show lines
of magnetic
force

Cardboard

Wire carrying
current

How can you increase the amount of magnetism on the cardboard? Use more wire, certainly.

EXPERIMENT 92

Materials: **Long piece of wire**

Sheet of cardboard

Switch

Dry cell

Iron filings

Punch a series of holes about an inch apart along two sides of the sheet of cardboard and run a length of wire around and around to form a series of loops.

Hook up the switch and dry cell and sprinkle iron filings along the cardboard where the wire goes through it. When you turn on the switch and tap the cardboard you will see the filings form into a circle around each wire. How can you make the

187

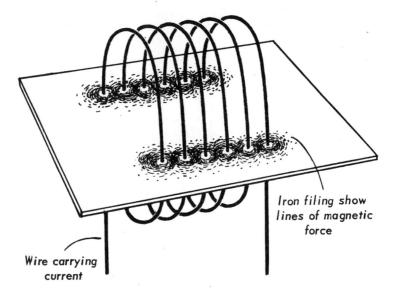

Iron filing show
lines of magnetic
force

Wire carrying
current

magnetic effect even stronger? By bringing as much
of the force of the magnetism together as you can
with a "magnetic funnel."

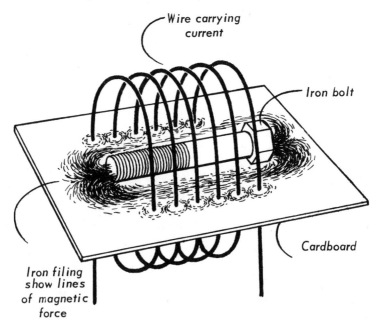

Wire carrying
current

Iron bolt

Cardboard

Iron filing
show lines
of magnetic
force

EXPERIMENT 93

Materials: The coil you just made

Iron bolt or nail

Slip the bolt through the center of the coils, add more iron filings—especially around the ends of the bolt—turn on the current and tap the cardboard.

The piece of iron pulls to it the lines of force of the magnetism around the wires and, in effect, increases the force of the magnetism at each end. You have just made an electric current go through a coil of wire wound around an iron core . . . and put together an electromagnet! Now for an electromagnet jumping jack.

EXPERIMENT 94

Materials: Wood

Copper wire

Nails

Switch

Dry cell

Mercury (or, as a substitute, very salty water)

Put the wooden pieces together so that the top piece is about 8 or 10 inches from the bottom piece. You can make the switch on the top of a strip about one inch wide cut from a tin can. Wrap the end of the spiral copper wire around the nail that goes clear through the top board. Make the wire just long enough for the straightened end to touch the pool of mercury in the bottom board. If you don't have any mercury, try very salty water. What you

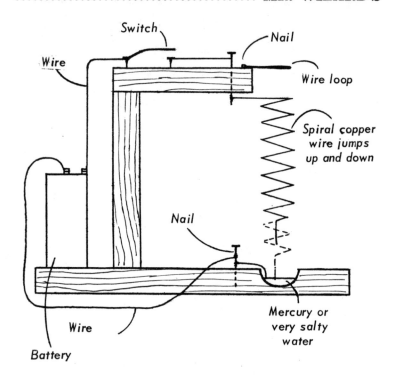

Switch

Nail

Wire

Wire loop

Spiral copper
wire jumps
up and down

Nail

Mercury or
very salty
water

Wire

Battery

want is a fluid that conducts electricity. Salt water may work, but mercury works better.

With the copper coil adjusted so the end just touches the surface of the fluid, trace the circuit before you close the switch. From the dry cell the current goes up the wire, through the switch and down the coils, through the fluid and back to the dry cell. When there is an electric current in the coils, however, magnetism is produced. The magnetism in the turns of the coil of wire is, let's say, "north" at the top of each turn and "south" at the bottom. North and south poles attract each other, so the turns of the coil are pulled together. This shortens the length of the coil and the straight wire at the bottom is pulled out of the fluid. Because this breaks

190

the flow of electricity, there's no longer any magnetism in the coil and it goes back to its original length. As soon as the straightened piece of wire touches the fluid, current can flow again and up goes the coil. When you've adjusted the various distances so they're just right, the wire jumps merrily up and down, sparking at the fluid with every jump. Now make it jump a lot higher.

EXPERIMENT 95

Materials: Electromagnetic jumping jack

Bolt

If you noticed, I suggested that you fasten a wire loop out from the end of the board on top. You had no use for it before, but now you can run the

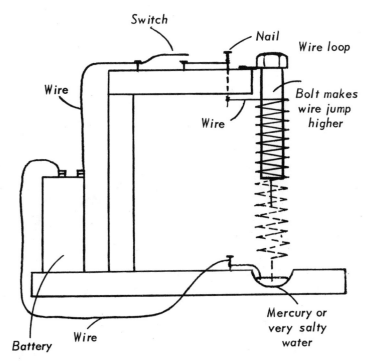

bolt through it so it hangs inside the loop.

The magnetic force is increased so much when you add the iron core to the electromagnet that the wire jumps about five times as high!

You don't have to go to all the trouble of making the wooden platform if you want to test the strength of an electromagnet. You can do it with a box of tacks.

EXPERIMENT 96

Materials: Insulated wire

Bolt or nail

Tape

Box of tacks (or pins, nails, etc.)

Starting a foot or so from one end of the wire,

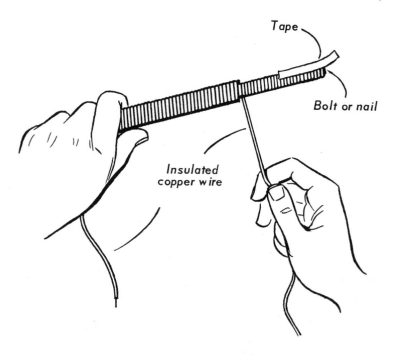

192

wind it carefully and neatly around the nail or bolt. Bell wire will do nicely. When you've covered the bolt completely with one layer of wire, start a second layer. Be sure to continue winding in the same direction. Use a piece of tape to hold the second layer in place.

You can add as many layers of wires as you can handle. The more layers, the stronger the magnetism will be. When you have finished winding the wire on the bolt, fasten the last turn securely with tape and connect the two ends of the wire through a switch to a battery. With the switch open, put one end of the electromagnet into the box of tacks and then out again. Not one tack comes out with it. Put the end of the bolt into the box of tacks again, turn on the current and raise the bolt. You'll probably pick up most of the tacks in the box!

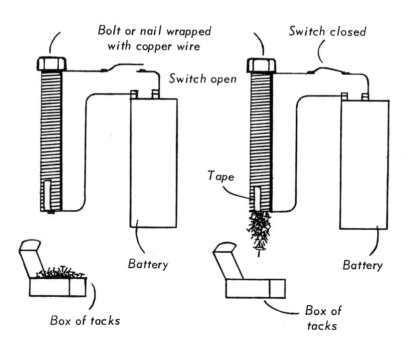

Bolt or nail wrapped with copper wire

Switch closed

Switch open

Tape

Battery

Battery

Box of tacks

Box of tacks

While you're holding up all the tacks, turn off the current. The tacks will drop to the table.

If you run the current through your electromagnet often enough, you'll find some of the tacks will remain sticking to the magnet after you've turned the current off. Why? Remember how you made a magnet out of a sewing needle? You stroked it with one side of a magnet and lined up the poles of the particles. That's what you're doing to the bolt too, but this time you're "stroking" it with magnetism in the wire when you turn on the electric current! You're gradually changing the bolt from a "temporary" magnet into a "permanent" one. Actually, since the bolt is soft iron, it cannot be permanently magnetized.

194

Now you're ready to make an electromagnet with which you can send messages. Here's how to make a hinge telegraph.

EXPERIMENT 97

Materials: **Wood**

Hinge

Large nail or screw

Switch

Wire

Dry cell

Nails

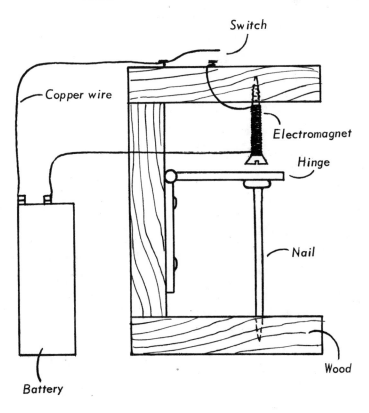

Put together a wooden frame like that shown. The height from top to bottom must be planned to allow from about $\frac{1}{4}$ to $\frac{3}{8}$ of an inch space between the hinge resting on the nail and the head of the screw. When you push down on the switch, an electric current is sent through the coils of wire around the screw. The electromagnetic screw pulls the hinge up with a "click." When you take your finger off the switch, the circuit is broken and the hinge drops back to the nail with another "click." With two fast clicks for a "dot" and two slower clicks for a "dash," you can send messages in Morse code. This is the way a real telegraph key and sounder work. But if you want to send messages that can be heard at a considerable distance, you want to make the tin-can telegraph.

EXPERIMENT 98

Materials: **Wood**

Bolt electromagnet you have already made

Tin can

Nails

Switch

Dry cell

Tape

Nail the can in place with the bottom facing the bolt electromagnet. Center the bolt on the bottom of the can and hold it into position on the wooden upright nailed to the base. Hook up the switch, dry cell and electromagnet, and with one hand hold the bolt very close to but not touching the bottom of the can. With the other hand press down on the switch. Adjust the distance between the end of the

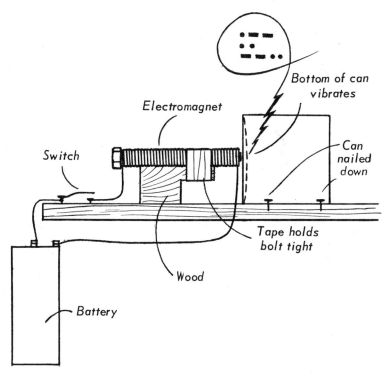

Bottom of can vibrates

Electromagnet

Switch

Can nailed down

Tape holds bolt tight

Wood

Battery

bolt and the bottom of the can carefully until you get the bottom of the can to vibrate. Release the switch and, without moving the bolt, tape it securely in that position. The can will vibrate with a penetrating sound as long as you hold the key (or switch) down. A short buzz is a "dot" and a longer buzz is a "dash."

EXPERIMENT 98-A

Materials: Morse code

So you can decode the message coming from the can in the drawing, and so you can send messages of your own, the letters and numbers of the Morse code are printed for you in a table on the following page.

A	·—	S	···
B	—···	T	—
C	—·—·	U	··—
D	—··	V	···—
E	·	W	·——
F	··—·	X	—··—
G	——·	Y	—·——
H	····	Z	——··
I	··	1	·————
J	·———	2	··———
K	—·—	3	···——
L	·—··	4	····—
M	——	5	·····
N	—·	6	—····
O	———	7	——···
P	·——·	8	———··
Q	——·—	9	————·
R	·—·	0	—————

Just to give you something to start with, here's a message in Morse code:

—·—— —— ··—
—·—· ·— —·
—— ·— —·— ·
·—
—··· ·· ·—— —··· —··· · ·—·
—· ···· ·— —
·—— —— ·—· —·— ···
·—·· ·· —·— ·
·—
—·· —— —— ·—· —··· · ·—·· ·—··

EXPERIMENT 99

Materials: **Pieces of wood**

Bolt or nail electromagnet

Strips of tin from a tin can

Nails

Screw

Tacks

Rubber band

Switch

Dry cell

Tools

The tricky part of this circuit is along the strip of "tin" cut from a tin can. It's actually iron covered with a thin layer of tin. This strip is held back by the rubber band at one end and touches the point of the screw at the other. You see, when you close the switch the electric current comes from the dry cell to the nail on which the strip pivots. It does this because it's curved around the nail. The electric current goes from the nail to the strip, along the strip to the point of the screw, through the screw

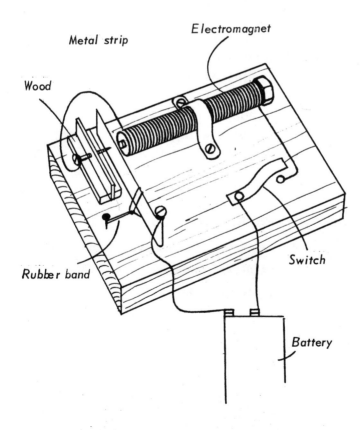

Metal strip

Electromagnet

Wood

Switch

Rubber band

Battery

and the wire connected to it, over to the wire coils of the electromagnet and then through the closed switch to the battery. This situation doesn't last very long because as soon as there is current in the coils of the electromagnet, the resulting magnetism pulls the strip away from the point of the screw. When this happens the circuit is broken at the point and no current flows through the electromagnet. That means there is no magnetic force pulling on the strip. The rubber band pulls the strip back until it touches the point of the screw and current flows once more. This "making" and "breaking" of the circuit happens so quickly that the strip vibrates with a buzzing sound. In a door bell the same thing happens, except there are two electromagnets hooked together for greater strength. A contact point is more efficient than the point of a screw. A little round hammer is attached to the strip, vibrates with it and taps against a metal bell.

Your friends know a table-tennis ball won't float at the end of a string like a circus balloon, but you can show them one that will . . . if you use a little electromagnetic "magic."

EXPERIMENT 100

Materials: **The best electromagnet you can make**

Cardboard box

Table-tennis ball

Paper clip

Thread

Switch

Dry cell

Connect the best electromagnet you can make to a dry cell and a switch. Hide the dry cell and switch under the table and the electromagnet inside the cardboard box. Cut a slit in the table-tennis ball just wide enough to push a paper clip inside. (Better test your paper clip first to make sure it's attracted by magnetism. I've found not all paper clips are made of iron or steel.) With the paper clip inside the ball, tie a bulky knot in the end of the thread and push it through the slit in the ball. Turn on the electromagnet and place the ball directly under it outside the box. The ball will be held to the bottom of the box because the magnetism attracts the paper clip. Pull on the thread from near the floor until the ball falls. It falls when you get the paper clip too far away from the magnet. Replace the ball and pull in the thread until you can find the greatest

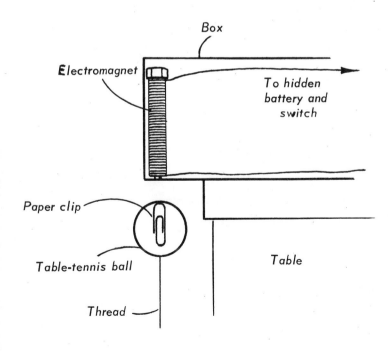

Box

Electromagnet

To hidden
battery and
switch

Paper clip

Table-tennis ball

Table

Thread

distance the ball can be from the box and still not fall. Tie the thread to any convenient weight on the floor with just enough length to hold the ball at the proper distance from the box. With the table-tennis ball on the floor and the dry cell and switch well but conveniently hidden, call in your friends and ask one to raise the ball as high as he can and let go. They're not going to be impressed when the ball falls. You say, "No. Not like that. Like this!" Secretly close the switch and raise the ball into position. Your friends are in for a surprise . . . especially when they reach for the ball only to have it fall to the floor before they can touch it. You've opened the switch, of course. Whether you explain to your friends how you do it is up to you.

If you have any friends who are very young, they will especially enjoy the electromagnetic dancing doll. If you don't have any very young friends, build the doll anyway, because friends of any age will enjoy watching her dance.

EXPERIMENT 101

Materials: Wood

Cardboard box

A good electromagnet

Wire from a coat hanger

Rubber bands

Paper clips

Paper doll

Switch

Dry cell

202

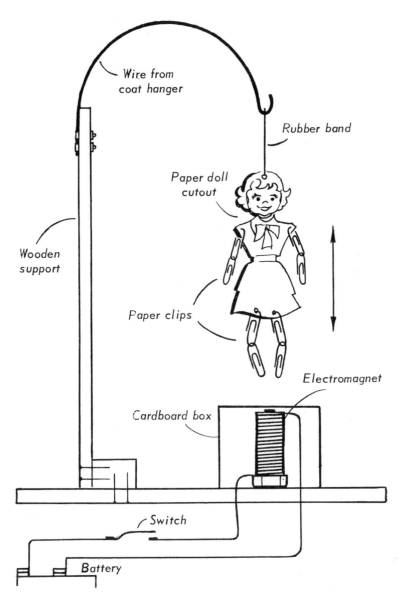

When you close the switch, Miss Paper Clip dances up and down under an electromagnetic "spell."

Chapter Eleven

Charge it!

HAVE YOU EVER stroked a piece of paper with a pencil? Not with the pointed end nor the eraser end, but like this:

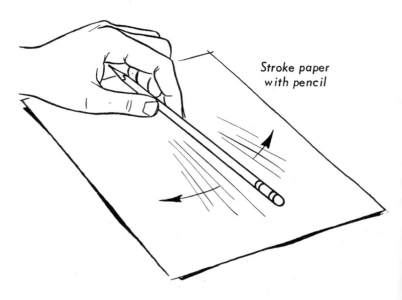

Stroke paper
with pencil

EXPERIMENT 102

Materials: Piece of paper

Pencil

If you have, you could have picked up the paper, smoothed it against the wall, and it would have stayed there!

Why would the paper have stayed on the wall? Because, without realizing it, you "made" electricity! To use that same kind of electricity in a more spectacular way, do this:

EXPERIMENT 103

Materials: Inflated rubber balloon

Piece of woolen cloth

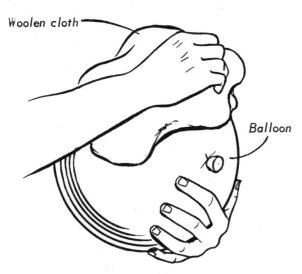

Rub an inflated rubber balloon with a piece of woolen cloth. You may have on a piece of woolen clothing; if so, simply rub the balloon against it.

Put the balloon against the wall and there it stays!

What kind of electricity is this, anyway? This mysterious kind of electricity you "make" when you rub a piece of paper with a pencil or a rubber balloon with a piece of woolen cloth is called "static" electricity. "Static" means "standing" in Greek. Static electricity is produced when two things are rubbed together. Some combinations of things work better than others: rubber and wool, silk and glass, silk and paper are all good pairs.

Incidentally, you'd best save the experiments in this chapter for a dry, cool day. Warm air has a lot of moisture in it and the static electricity you "make" "leaks" off rapidly to the moisture. You can try the experiments any time, but if you're not too successful wait for a change in the weather.

Why a table-tennis ball follows a comb around will be understandable now that you know something about static electricity.

Rub pocket comb with woolen cloth

EXPERIMENT 104

Materials: **Hard-rubber comb**

Table-tennis ball

Piece of woolen cloth

Rub the comb vigorously with the woolen cloth. The comb is now electrically charged. Bring it near a table-tennis ball lying on the table. The neutral ball will roll to the comb. Keep moving the comb ahead of the ball and you can keep rolling it all over the top of the table.

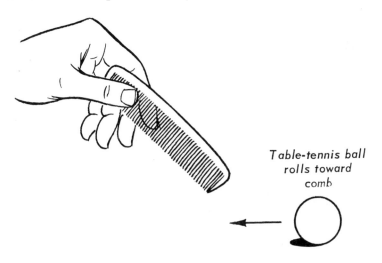

Table-tennis ball rolls toward comb

EXPERIMENT 105

Materials: **Hard-rubber comb**

Piece of woolen cloth

Stream of water from a faucet

Ever see a bent stream of water coming out of a faucet?

Turn on the faucet until you can get the smallest stream possible without it breaking into drops.

Rub the comb briskly with the wool and bring it close to, but not touching, the stream of water from the faucet. As the water falls, it bends towards the comb!

The stream of water is neutral and, therefore, attracted to the electrically charged comb. Your friends who might have seen a balloon stick to a wall will probably not have seen a bent stream of water coming out of a faucet . . . until you show them.

What about you? Are you neutral enough to attract a balloon?

EXPERIMENT 106

Materials: **Inflated balloon**

Piece of woolen cloth

Rub the balloon with the wool. When Betsy brought the balloon close to her face it stuck to her cheek, proving she was "neutral."

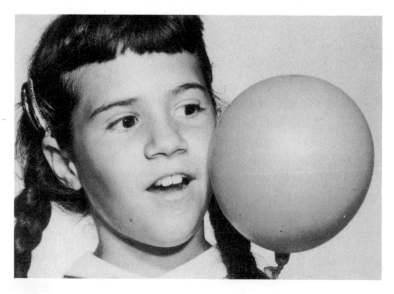

EXPERIMENT 107

Materials: Three inflated balloons tied up with long strings

Piece of woolen cloth

Tie the three strings together and suspend the balloons so they hang down in a bunch. Rub each one with the wool and watch them waltz around each other.

Each balloon is negatively charged when you rub it with the wool, and from the way they avoid each other, you can be pretty sure "like charges repel." You'd think there must be some way of getting these like charges to be more friendly . . . and there is.

EXPERIMENT 108

Materials: Sheet of newspaper

Scissors

Piece of silk cloth

Ruler or stick

Open up a double sheet of newspaper with a fold down the middle. Cut a four-inch strip from across the top. Lay this strip on the table and stroke it with the silk cloth. You're charging the paper with positive electricity and the silk with negative electricity. Hold the ruler in one hand and with the other drape the paper strip over the ruler.

Both ends of the paper hanging down are positively charged and, instead of hanging straight down, repel each other and rise out to each side.

Bring your hand in between the ends of the paper and they'll close in on your hand.

Recall that "positive charges attract neutral." Your neutral hand attracts both the positively

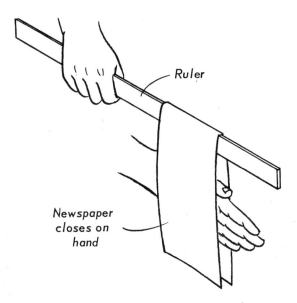

Ruler

Newspaper closes on hand

charged ends of the paper at the same time. Just offering them your hand brought them together and made them "friends."

Sometimes, though, things get too friendly as far as electrical charges go, and the friendship is broken up in all directions at once.

EXPERIMENT 109

Materials: Hard-rubber comb

Piece of woolen cloth

A cork

A coarse file

File the end of a cork with a coarse file until you get a pile of small cork filings. Rub the comb with the wool and put the comb into the pile of cork filings. Raise the comb and many of the little pieces of cork will cling to it. The pieces of cork in the pile are neutral, and when you bring the negatively

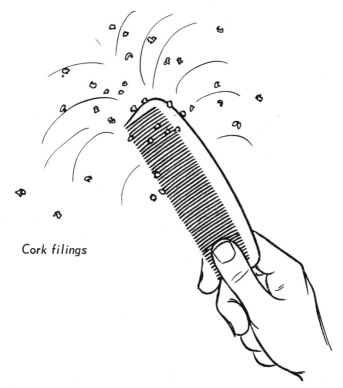

Cork filings

charged comb near them they are attracted to it. But they won't remain "friends" for long. As soon as they get a negative charge too, they jump away from the comb.

This makes sense when you realize that unlike charges attract and like charges repel.

Now put the same idea to work in a "square dance."

EXPERIMENT 110

Materials: **Pane of glass**

Aluminum pie plate

Piece of soft leather

Tissue paper

211

Out of the tissue paper cut four men and four women like these:

About
1 inch·

Small figures cut from tissue paper

They should be slightly shorter than the depth of the pie plate . . . usually about an inch. Put the men and women on the bottom of the aluminum pie plate and cover them with the pane of glass. With the piece of soft leather rub the top surface of the

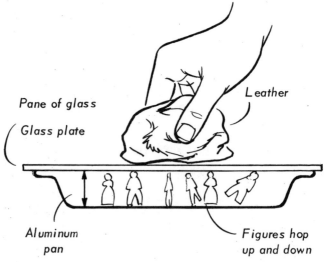

Pane of glass

Glass plate

Leather

Aluminum
pan

Figures hop
up and down

212

glass. The men and women will hop up and down.

The "square dancing" is a result of the negative charge you put on the glass. This charge attracts the neutral figures. They jump up to the glass where they become negatively charged too and jump back down to the pan. If it's not exactly square dancing, it's as close as you'll ever get to it with static electricity!

I suppose you have rubbed your feet as you walked across a thick woolen carpet and felt a spark jump when you brought your finger near a metal object. You understand now that when you rubbed your feet on the woolen carpet you gave yourself a negative charge which was discharged quickly when you brought it near that metal object. You heard and felt the quick discharge as a spark. I doubt if you ever felt a spark an inch long, though. Willy has.

EXPERIMENT 111

Materials: **Two people**

Four drinking glasses

Piece of fur

Large metal object

Arrange the four drinking glasses in a tight square upside down on the floor near a large metal object. Have one person stand on the glasses. Have the other person hit him on the back twenty or thirty times with the piece of fur. When the person standing on the glasses brings his finger near the metal object, a long spark will jump . . . and so will he. The length of the spark will be greatest on a cold, clear, winter day. While you're waiting for

such a day to come along, look at Willy as Betsy
beat him on the back for science . . . and a one-inch
spark.

Chapter Twelve

The wonders of water

STRICTLY SPEAKING, you wouldn't call these three things "wonderful," would you?

And yet an ice cube, a glass of water and a kettle of boiling water *are* full of wonders. Water is a most amazing material. It's probably the only thing you've ever known in all three of its physical forms: as a solid (ice), as a liquid (water), and as a gas (steam). Most other things can be made into solids, liquids and gases. But have you ever seen, say, iron, gasoline or air in all three forms? Probably not. But the three forms of water are as commonplace as your kitchen . . . the place where you can marvel at the wonders of ice, water and steam. Start with a puzzle concerning an ice cube from the refrigerator.

EXPERIMENT 112

Materials: **Ice cube**

String

Glass of water

The secret from the cellar (magic ingredient)

Here's the puzzle: when you float the ice cube in the water, how are you going to get it out again, using the string but no knots and without touching the ice cube with your fingers?

Your first thought may be to form a loop in the string and lift the ice cube out. If you think a second, though, you will realize how impossible that is because you'll have to keep the center of gravity directly over the string. You know that because you found out "why balance gets lost" in Chapter 5. As you might expect, there is a science secret—and it's in the cellar. Here's how to pick up the ice cube with the string: wet the end of the string thoroughly in water in the glass and lay it on top of

the ice cube. Along the top of the cube, on each side of the string, sprinkle salt.

That's the secret from the cellar ... a salt cellar! Wait a half a minute or so and you can raise the ice cube out of the glass with the string because it's now frozen to the ice cube!

If you know why people sprinkle salt on icy sidewalks you know why the string is frozen to the ice cube.

You know water turns to ice at 32 degrees above zero Fahrenheit. But if water has salt (or other materials, for that matter) dissolved in it, its temperature has to go below 32 degrees before it changes to ice. When you sprinkle salt on the ice cube, it begins to dissolve in the water on top of the ice cube. The salt water is at about 32 degrees but it won't freeze until it gets colder. The water on the string is a lot warmer because you dipped it in the water in the glass. The heat in the water on the string flows to the salt water and the temperature of the water on the string begins to drop. Before long it has lost so much heat that the temperature gets down to 32 degrees. It's not salt water, so it freezes to the ice cube. That's when you can pick up the other end of the string and raise the ice cube out of the glass!

People sprinkle salt on icy sidewalks so the salt

will take heat away from the ice, raise the temperature above freezing and melt it. This works out fine as long as the temperature outside isn't so low that the salt water freezes too. If that's the case, they're just wasting salt.

You took for granted that the ice cube would float in the water. Isn't that amazing? No? Well, it is. The next time you melt a solid, notice that as it turns to a liquid the solid stays on the bottom. When you melt shortening, paraffin, butter, lead, solder . . . all the solid pieces stay on the *bottom* of the liquid but not solid water. It floats!

And think about this: you know that convection currents in water are the result of colder water going down and pushing the warmer water up. You expect the colder water to be at the bottom of a pond, and you feel it there when you dive down to the bottom when you're in swimming in the summer. In winter then, why doesn't this colder water freeze first and form ice on the bottom of the lake? That's what ought to happen, but it doesn't!

Here's why water changing into ice is a won-

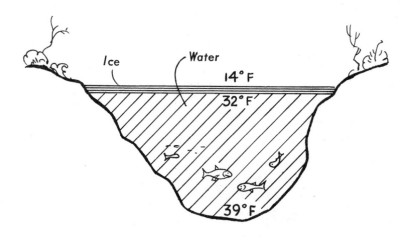

derful thing. When other things lose heat or cool off they contract or get smaller and heavier. Water does this too. As its temperature drops, it gets heavier and heavier until it reaches the temperature of 39 degrees above zero Fahrenheit. Then a strange reversal takes place. At 39 degrees, water begins to expand and get lighter. As its temperature continues to drop it gets lighter yet until, at 32 degrees, it's at its lightest. Water won't get any colder than this because when any more heat is taken away from it it changes to ice which expands even further! That's why the ice cube floats in your glass. It weighs less than an equal volume of water. And that's why a pond doesn't freeze from the bottom up like it ought to.

If you want to prove to yourself that ice floats because it expands as it changes from water, do this:

EXPERIMENT 113

Materials: Glass bottle with metal screw top

Water

A cold day

When it's good and cold outside, fill the bottle with cold water to the very top and screw on the top tightly. Put it outside in a safe place. As the water changes to ice, the ice will take up more room because it expands. But there is no more room in the bottle. The ice will push against the inside of the bottle hard enough to break it. You had better anticipate this and put the bottle where the pieces of broken glass won't do any damage.

EXPERIMENT 114

Materials: Snow

While you're putting the bottle outside, scoop up enough snow to make a snowball. You pat and press it as you turn it to make it into a ball.

If you keep on doing this you'll end up with a hard snowball with a smooth layer of thin ice around it. You've done that many times without thinking about it if you live where there is snow. Where did the layer of ice come from?

And why is it, when you take the ice cubes out of the refrigerator tray and put them in a dish, the cubes sometimes freeze together? They ought to be melting and here they are freezing! This experiment will answer both questions.

EXPERIMENT 115

Materials: **Ice cube**

Thin wire

Piece of wood

Heavy weight

The piece of wood should be slightly narrower than the ice cube is long. Fasten one end of the piece of wood to a support like a table with nails, clamps or a heavy weight or any other way you want to, so that the other end of the wood sticks out over the support. Place an ice cube on that end of the piece of wood and support a fairly heavy weight off the floor with a thin wire looped over the ice cube.

The size of the weight and the thickness of the wire determine how long it will be before the wire goes right through the ice cube without cutting it in half! There's a magic trick for you, as amazing as a magician sawing a lady in half. The magician uses trickery while you use simple science.

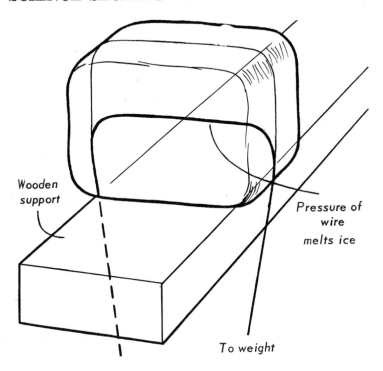

Wooden
support

Pressure of
wire
melts ice

To weight

You saw what happened to the bottle of water when it changed to ice so you know that ice gets bigger as it freezes. If you forced it to get smaller again it should melt and change to water. Logical enough. How can you make the ice smaller? By putting pressure on it. That's exactly what you do with the wire supporting the weight off the floor. All of the force of gravity pulling on the weight is concentrated on the wire resting on the ice cube. The pressure of the wire changes the solid ice directly under it to liquid water. The liquid flows from under the wire, up around it and the wire then rests on ice again. The pressure starts to change that ice to water. This process continues and the wire moves slowly down through the ice cube.

221

But what happens to the water that's above the wire as it moves down? As soon as the pressure is released, it changes back to ice again. And that's the simple science of how to cut an ice cube in half without cutting it in half!

What are you doing when you "pack" a snowball? Putting pressure on the little crystals of ice called "snow," and changing some of them to water. When you let up on the pressure, the water freezes and you eventually get a real "cannon ball."

What happens when you pile ice cubes in a dish? They're pushed together and the pressure on the sides of the ice cube changes part of each one to water. The water runs down to the bottom of the dish, the pressure is released and the two surfaces of the ice cubes freeze together.

And now you'll understand perfectly when I say that you don't skate on ice but on water! The weight of your body, pressing down on the small area of the runners of your skates, melts the ice underneath and you glide along on a thin film of water. As soon as you pass by the water promptly changes back to ice. Melting snow for icy snowballs or ice into water for skating, with pressure, works fine as long as the snow or ice isn't too cold. The colder the snow or ice is, the more pressure it takes to change them to water. That's why a very cold day is no day for making snowballs or going skating. You can't have fun doing either unless you can put on the pressure and get water.

Assuming it's been cold enough—but not too cold—for snowballs and skating and that you've tired yourself out with "experimenting" on both, how about a dish of hot buttered popcorn?

EXPERIMENT 116

Materials: **Popcorn**

              Popcorn popper

              Butter

              Salt

You won't need any directions for popping the popcorn, so go right ahead. You may not have as much success, though, figuring out the answer to this real-life riddle as you watch the popcorn pop; "*Why* does it pop?" One moment it's a little brown seed and the next moment it explodes into a fluffy white "flower." You might have guessed it's because of that wonderful water again.

You see, a kernel of popcorn *is* a seed—a seed that has food and water inside of it and a tough shell around it. When you heat the seed the water inside gets hotter and hotter until it suddenly "blows up." It's not a liquid any more, it's a gas called "steam." That steam expands so much and so fast

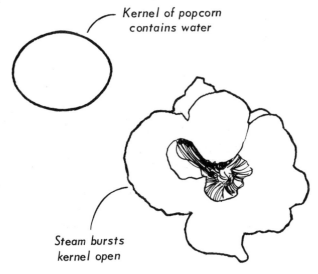

Kernel of popcorn
contains water

Steam bursts
kernel open

it bursts open the hard shell of the seed and puffs up the food inside.

What happens to make water "blow up" and become steam?

We haven't talked about molecules yet but we ought to because they've very important to scientists . . . and to you. Molecules are part of another theory scientists have developed and here's a part of what that theory is.

Everything in the world is made up of molecules: the air, the land, the water, the trees, your house, even you, are just a bunch of molecules. Molecules are the smallest pieces of anything that it would be possible to get. The smallest piece of water, for instance, is a water molecule. The water molecule is made up of even smaller pieces called atoms, but to get them you would have to take the water molecules apart and then it's not water any more. These water molecules are far too small to see, even with a very powerful microscope, but scientists have found out a lot about them without actually seeing them. They know, for example, that all molecules are moving about, and one of the things that keeps them moving is heat energy. The more heat you add to the moving molecules, the more they move. That's why water (and almost everything else) can be changed to a solid or a gas. It all depends on how much heat is making the molecules move. The relatively little heat in ice means the molecules can't move very much. They stick pretty close together and form a "solid." With more heat added, however, they move further apart. This means they can move around without bumping into each other as often. They flow because they're now a liquid. It actually takes heat to change ice at 32 degrees above zero Fahrenheit to water at 32 degees. The extra heat doesn't raise the temperature at all. It simply pushes the molecules from their solid distances to their liquid distances.

The water molecules continue to move further apart as more heat is added. Molecules of warm water are further apart than those of cold water. (Think back to those convection currents in Chapter 6.) The distance between molecules continues to increase until the temperature of the water gets to 212 degrees above zero Fahrenheit. More heat at this temperature and the "blowing up" occurs. The added heat pushes the molecules really far apart. They zoom out in all directions. If more heat is added to the water at 212 degrees, it won't get any hotter but more molecules will zoom into steam. The water is being changed from a liquid to a gas and the water molecules are pushed from their liquid distances to their gas distances. While you can't see water molecules, you can see what a difference heat makes in changing them from their liquid form to their gas form.

EXPERIMENT 117

Materials: Glass cooking pot

Water

Heat

Put water in the pot and get it to boiling. Look at the water in the bottom of the pot. Don't you see something like this?

The heat is changing the liquid water to steam. The steam expands and forms bubbles on the bottom

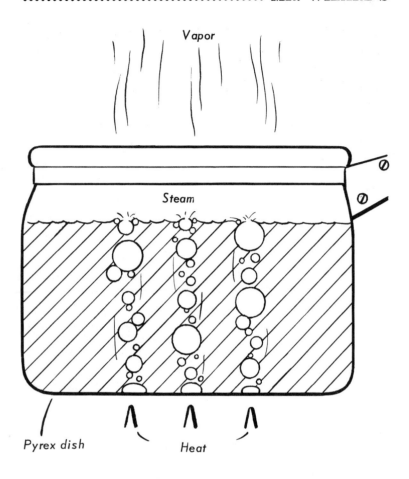

Vapor

Steam

Pyrex dish

Heat

which rise to the top of the water. There is a layer right above the water where you can't see anything. That's where the steam is. You can't see it because the molecules are so far apart you see right between them!

Above the layer of invisible steam are clouds of white stuff. These clouds form when the steam cools off and condenses back into small droplets of water. When there are enough of these little droplets grouped together in the air you can see them.

Now that you know what happens when water "blows up" to steam, you won't be surprised to know that you can boil water in a paper box.

EXPERIMENT 118

Materials: Light-weight cardboard or heavy paper

    Paper clips

    Water

    Heat

Fold the paper at the corners and fasten the corners to form this kind of a box.

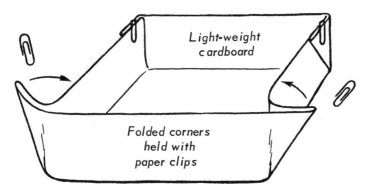

Light-weight cardboard

Folded corners held with paper clips

Add more than enough water to cover the bottom of the box and set it on the stove. As soon as the water gets hot enough it boils . . . but the paper box does not burn!

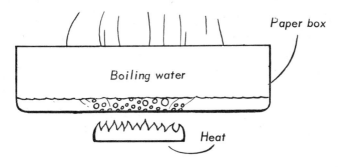

Paper box

Boiling water

Heat

The heat from the stove flows through the bottom of the paper box and then to the water. The water in the paper box can't get any hotter than 212 degrees Fahrenheit because then it changes to steam. All the heat coming through the paper is absorbed by the water and that means the box is kept at 212 degrees Fahrenheit. In order to burn, however, the paper has to get hotter than that. This won't happen as long as there is water in the box. When all the water is boiled away the heat will raise the temperature of the box quickly. Be prepared to put out a burning box.

Some people go all the way to Yellowstone Park to look at "Old Faithful." If all they wanted to see was a geyser in action they should have gone to their kitchen instead. Have you got a geyser in your kitchen?

EXPERIMENT 119

Materials: **Deep, wide cooking dish**

Funnel

Nail

Water

Heat

Fill the dish part way full of water, lay the nail on the bottom and put the funnel over the nail. When the water boils, the bubbles of steam are collected by the funnel. When a lot of them come together all at once near the neck of the funnel, they push the water in the neck out ahead of them. The water shoots out, the steam escapes and more water flows into the funnel through the space provided by the nail.

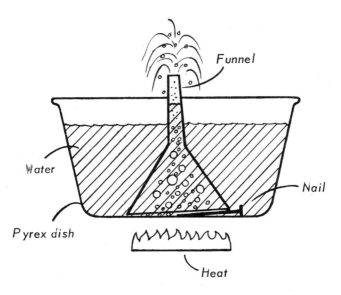

Funnel

Water

Nail

Pyrex dish

Heat

This is the way Old Faithful works. The heat and water are underground and the water shoots high into the air at regular intervals. With that explanation of how a geyser works as a clue, you should be able to spot the one in your kitchen.

EXPERIMENT 120

Materials: **Percolator**

Water

Heat

Put the coffee on and when it's perking, save the trip to Yellowstone: you've got a geyser in your kitchen.

There are many, many more wonders of water: solid, liquid or gas. You've looked at only a few of them. We'll have to save the rest for another book. But I hope you appreciate how marvelous it is the next time you drink a glass of "the wonderful stuff."

Chapter Thirteen

Bubbles at work

YOU'VE SEEN LOTS OF BUBBLES, I suppose, but have you ever put them to work? Let's put bubbles to work right now in an antiaircraft cannon. Do this experiment outside so you won't hit the ceiling with the shell.

EXPERIMENT 121

Materials: Soda bottle

Cork

Tissue paper

Vinegar

Sodium bicarbonate

Measuring cup

Teaspoon

Scissors

Water

Make a solution of half vinegar and half water in the measuring cup. Pour it into the soda bottle. Cut strips of tissue paper and attach them to the cork with a thumbtack. Cut out a piece of tissue paper about four inches by four inches and lay it on the table. In the middle of the paper put a teaspoon full of sodium bicarbonate (you may know it as bicarbonate of soda or baking soda, but the chemist calls it sodium bicarbonate, so you call it that too).

Roll the tissue up into a tube with the soda inside. Twist the ends to keep the soda from falling out and put it in the bottle. Put the cork into the mouth of the bottle.

The bottle is an antiaircraft cannon and the cork is the shell. The shell is going to be shot out of the cannon with a report. You don't want to shoot down a light fixture, and that's why you should put the charge in your cannon out of doors. Don't worry,

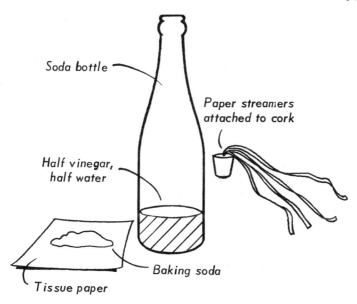

Soda bottle

Paper streamers attached to cork

Half vinegar, half water

Tissue paper

Baking soda

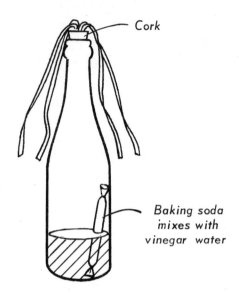

Cork

Baking soda
mixes with
vinegar water

the bottle cannon is not particularly dangerous because here's what happens.

When the vinegar solution (acid) wets the tissue paper, it reacts with the sodium bicarbonate (base) and a chemical reaction begins. One of the results is a gas called "carbon dioxide." You can see the bubbles of gas in the solution. They rise to the surface, break and begin to build up pressure inside the bottle. When the pressure gets great enough the cork is shot out of the bottle with a loud pop. You see, under the right conditions bubbles can do plenty of work. When you change the conditions slightly, they will help you make a fountain.

EXPERIMENT 122

Materials: Soda bottle

One-hole stopper

Glass tube

Vinegar

Sodium bicarbonate

Water

Tissue paper

This time fill the bottle three-fourths full of water and vinegar solution. Arrange the glass tubing and cork as shown but before you put it in the bottle, toss in the sodium bicarbonate rolled in the tissue paper. As soon as the chemical reaction starts the pressure of the carbon-dioxide gas on top of the solution will force it up through the glass tube out into the air in a spectacular fountain!

233

The bubbles of carbon dioxide do more useful work for you than just shooting a cork out of a bottle or making a fountain. Take griddle cakes, for instance. You won't get light, tasty griddle cakes without the work of carbon-dioxide bubbles. Quiz: find the ingredients that make the carbon dioxide.

EXPERIMENT 123

Materials: (Recipe for sour-milk griddle cakes)

$2\frac{1}{2}$ cups flour

$\frac{1}{2}$ teaspoon salt

1 egg

$1\frac{1}{4}$ teaspoons soda

2 tablespoons butter

2 cups sour milk

Watch the cakes on the griddle. You'll see bubbles work their way to the top surface. The carbon dioxide is puffing up the batter and the heat is cooking it. Did you pick the carbon-dioxide makers in the recipe? Soda is another name for sodium bicarbonate and when milk sours, it becomes slightly acid. Soda plus acid produces carbon dioxide! The next time you eat a piece of cake, examine it. You'll find it's full of holes.

The holes were made by bubbles of carbon dioxide again; made with slightly different ingredients this time. Quiz: find the carbon-dioxide-producing ingredients in this cake recipe:

EXPERIMENT 124

Materials: (Recipe for making sponge cake)

4 eggs

1 cup sugar

¾ cup water

1½ cups flour

3 teaspoons baking powder

1 teaspoon vanilla

Bake the cake if you can and see the bubbles for yourself. If you assumed the baking powder has sodium bicarbonate in it, you were right. But where's the acid? It's in the baking powder too! Baking powder is a combination of powders that are both base and acid. When the powders are in the can there's little, if any, water around. They're simply mixed together without actually combining in a chemical reaction. However, when you mix the baking powder with water, the powders dissolve and a chemical reaction starts that sets carbon-dioxide gas free. Most cakes rise because carbon-dioxide bubbles are hard at work inside of them. There are exceptions, and one you should know about is angel-food cake. It's made with the whites of about a dozen eggs. The cook whips or beats the egg whites full of air bubbles before putting the cake in the oven. The batter is hardened by the heat before the air has a chance to escape and let the cake fall. So even in an angel-food cake . . . bubbles are at work.

You can see baking powder making carbon-dioxide bubbles and make a delicious looking "soda fountain" at the same time. You can't eat it, unfortunately.

EXPERIMENT 125

Materials: Glass

Baking powder

Dish

Spoon

Water

Put four heaping teaspoons of baking powder in the glass. Set it in the dish. Add enough water to moisten the baking powder thoroughly and stir.

Very soon the chemical reaction starts and the "soda fountain" will flow over the sides and run down the stem of the glass into the dish.

236

The bubbles are filled with that hard-working gas, carbon dioxide.

The bubbles you get in a real soda that you buy at a soda fountain are filled with carbon-dioxide gas too. No baking powder is used to get them, though. You'll find out where they come from a little later.

You've seen the holes in griddle cakes and sponge cake. How about the holes in bread? Carbon dioxide is responsible for them too. That's what makes the bread rise. Where does the carbon dioxide come from in this list of ingredients for bread?

EXPERIMENT 126

Materials: (Recipe for making bread)
  Flour
  Yeast
  Water
  Salt

Maybe you know that bread rises because of the yeast. But how does the yeast, which is a form of plant, give you carbon dioxide? When the yeast plants begin to grow and multiply in the dough, one of the byproducts of their living process is carbon-dioxide gas. The bubbles produced by the yeast plant make the dough rise. You can make bread without yeast, but then you shouldn't call it bread. You should call it "hardtack." It would be almost as hard as a tack, too, because without carbon-dioxide bubbles working away inside, the dough doesn't rise. -

You see how hard bubbles work for you? They do all sorts of odd jobs. To be a good scientist, however, you can't just let them do their work without knowing more about the gas inside of them. Carbon-dioxide gas is fun to investigate. You can make a supply of it in a generator like this.

EXPERIMENT 127

Materials: **Soda bottle**

Vinegar

Water

Sodium bicarbonate

One-hole stopper

Glass tube

Rubber tube

Tissue paper

Set up the materials as shown and when the chemical reaction starts coming out of the rubber

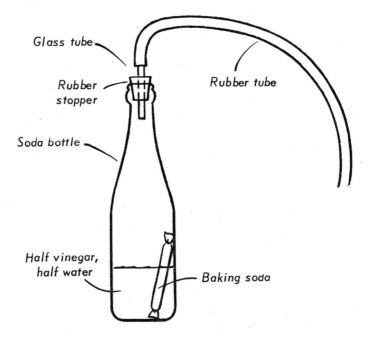

Glass tube

Rubber stopper

Rubber tube

Soda bottle

Half vinegar, half water

Baking soda

tube, you'll have a handy supply of carbon dioxide gas. First, let's weigh it.

EXPERIMENT 128

Materials: **Carbon-dioxide gas generator**

Identical paper bags

Stick

String

Balance the stick with the string tied around the center of it and hang from any convenient place. At each end of the stick tie a paper bag. Adjust the bags so they balance. Are the bags empty? No, they're full of air. Now fill one bag with carbon-dioxide gas from your generator. It will be hard to tell if any gas is coming out of the rubber tube because carbon-dioxide gas is invisible. But if there

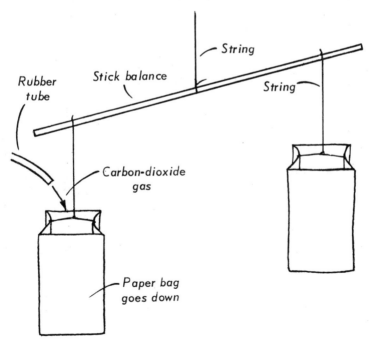

Rubber tube

Stick balance

String

String

Carbon-dioxide gas

Paper bag goes down

are bubbles in the solution in the bottle generator, you know you're getting carbon dioxide out of the tube.

You'll know you're pouring carbon-dioxide gas into the bag when it starts to sink. Carbon dioxide is heavier than air and when you get enough of it into the bag, the stick balance will show it. That's very important information as you'll see in a moment.

Why is this gas called "carbon dioxide?" It's called that because it's a combination of carbon and oxygen. Now you'd think if carbon dioxide contains oxygen that things would burn in it just like they do in air which also contains oxygen. Well, make this test.

EXPERIMENT 129

Materials: **Carbon-dioxide generator**

Water

Glass

Wire

Candle

Matches

Fasten the candle to the wire so you can lower it into the glass when it's lighted. Fill the glass about half full of carbon-dioxide gas . . . as nearly as you can guess at it. Light the candle and slowly lower it into the glass. When the flame reaches the gas, it will go out showing you that, in spite of the fact that carbon dioxide has oxygen in it, the oxygen does not leave the carbon. They stay together as carbon dioxide. The candle goes out because it can't get any oxygen. Way back in Chapter 3 you poured carbon-dioxide gas down a paper trough and put out a candle. Remember?

Now for a trick. Light the candle again and slowly lower it into the glass. Go down very slowly until the flame starts to leave the wick. You'll have the flame burning ¾ of an inch from the end of the wick!

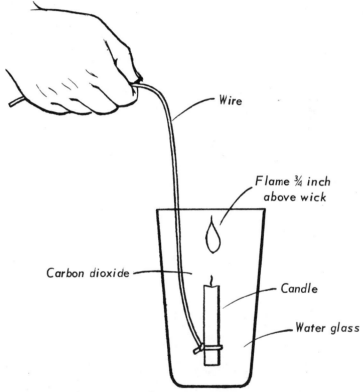

Wire

Flame ¾ inch above wick

Carbon dioxide

Candle

Water glass

The hot gases are still coming from the candle wick, but can't burn because the carbon dioxide keeps the oxygen away. The hot gases rise through the layer of carbon dioxide and emerge into the oxygen above it, still hot enough to burn.

You can make it even more tricky-looking by using three candles.

EXPERIMENT 130

Materials: **Carbon-dioxide gas generator**

Three candles of different lengths

Matches

A deep glass bowl

Stand the candles apart in the bowl, light them and then hold the end of the tube of the carbon-dioxide gas generator over the edge of the bowl. The candles will go out one at a time from the bottom up. The heavier-than-air carbon-dioxide gas fills up the bowl and as it reaches the level of each candle flame, out goes the flame!

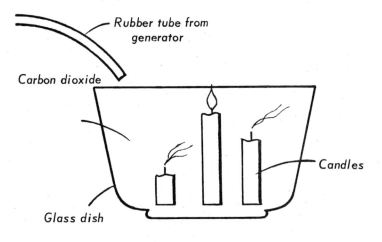

Rubber tube from generator

Carbon dioxide

Candles

Glass dish

EXPERIMENT 131

Materials: **Milk bottle**

Vinegar

Sodium bicarbonate

Water

Small bottle

Because carbon-dioxide gas puts out fire so readily, it's used in lots of fire extinguishers. You can combine the pressure of your soda-bottle fountain with the generator and make a carbon-dioxide fire extinguisher of your own.

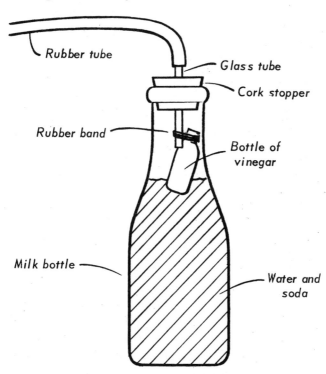

When you turn your home-made fire extinguisher sideways or upside down you can see what happens. The vinegar in the little bottle spills out and combines with the soda already dissolved in the water. The pressure that results when the gas is formed forces the water out of the tube a lot further than just plain gravity could. And besides, the water is filled with carbon-dioxide gas. Water and carbon-dioxide gas are both good fire fighters.

You can refine your fire extinguisher by adding a glass nozzle like that from a glass medicine dropper, by using half vinegar and half water below and by fastening the roll of tissue paper with the sodium bicarbonate in it to the top. The reason I suggested you make it the other way around is because then you've made one that works exactly like a real one.

You've seen fire extinguishers like this in schools, office buildings, factories and lots of other places. It's more efficient than yours because it's bigger, holds more water, and, instead of vinegar, it uses sulphuric acid, which is very powerful. To use the extinguisher you either turn a handle or simply turn it upside down just like you did yours.

Can you see any bubbles of carbon dioxide in front of your nose? Of course not. But there's carbon dioxide there just the same! Every time you breathe out a portion of the air that comes out of your nose is carbon dioxide. There's a "slow burning" going on inside of you because your body uses oxygen to combine with food and "burn" it for energy. One of the products of this oxidizing is your tried-and-true friend in the bubbles—carbon dioxide.

Whenever you combine oxygen with anything that's got carbon in it, whether you do it quickly with heat and light being given off and call it burning, or do it slowly with little heat and no light and call it oxidizing, carbon dioxide is one of the results. Take a burning match, for instance. The wood is a combination of, among other things, hydrogen and carbon. When the wood burns this is what happens to the various materials:

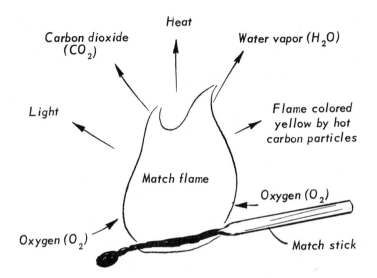

The chemist uses symbols to stand for various substances. It's kind of like a chemical shorthand. H_2O means water; O_2 means oxygen; CO_2 means carbon dioxide.

If you find it hard to believe that a gas can be dissolved in water . . . try this.

EXPERIMENT 132

Materials: Bottle of pop, soda, root beer or any soft drink

Bottle opener

Open the bottle and watch what happens near the top of the liquid.

The bubbles you see are . . . yes, carbon dioxide. It was dissolved in the water just like the flavoring is. The liquid in the bottle is under pressure when the cap is on and that keeps the CO_2 dissolved in the water. When you take the cap off, the pressure is released and the carbon dioxide comes out of solution ("un-dissolved" is just not the way to say it) and rises to the top as bubbles. You can feel those bubbles when you drink the pop. Doesn't it fizz as you swallow it? You're heating the liquid up slightly and shaking it about and that makes more CO_2 come out of solution. The bubbles burst in your mouth and throat and sometimes "tickle" your nose.

When you made the "soda fountain" that looked like an ice-cream soda but wasn't, you made carbon-dioxide bubbles with baking powder. Here's how the man behind the soda fountain uses CO_2 bubbles.

EXPERIMENT 133

Materials: The makings of an ice-cream soda

(If they're not handy, a glass of water with

CO_2 dissolved in it: pop, soda water, etc.)

Pour a glass of soda water and note how fast the bubbles of CO_2 form. Now add a teaspoon of sugar without stirring. You'll see many more bubbles form quickly as the sugar dissolves with the water and the CO_2 comes out of solution.

Have you ever seen mothballs dance? They will with the help of carbon-dioxide gas dissolved in water.

EXPERIMENT 134

Materials: Glass

Water

Vinegar

Sodium bicarbonate

Teaspoon

Mothballs

Piece of soap

Add a half a cup or so of vinegar to a half a glass of water. Put four or five (not too many, now) mothballs in the glass. Because they're heavier than an equal volume of water, they sink. Now stir in thoroughly a teaspoon of sodium bicarbonate. Because the sodium bicarbonate dissolves in the water, the reaction that produces the CO_2 bubbles will last quite a while. For a very short while, the carbon dioxide is dissolved in water until more gas is generated than the water can hold. Then the bubbles of CO_2 form . . . especially on the little points of the mothballs. The mothballs are heavier than water, but the bubbles of carbon dioxide clinging on them are lighter than water. Soon there are enough bubbles to lift the mothballs slowly right to the top of the water. There the bubbles of CO_2 burst into the air, making the top of the mothballs heavier than the bottom, where there are still bubbles. This makes the mothballs top heavy. They roll over, breaking more bubbles into the air as they do so. The loss of so many bubbles makes them heavier than water again and they slowly sink to the bottom. But the gas is still coming out of solution and the bubbles begin to form on the mothballs all over again. While some mothballs are on the way up, others are on the way down. Such "dancing" mothballs you've never seen.

Chapter Fourteen

The biggest mystery of all — you!

YOU'VE BEEN INVESTIGATING the mysteries all around you, now let's investigate you. In many ways you're the biggest mystery of all. As you go about your daily life you do things so automatically you never stop to think about why or how you do them. Take the simple act of getting out of a chair.

EXPERIMENT 135

Materials: A chair

Sit up straight, well back in the chair, with your feet flat on the floor in front of you. Without moving your body forward or your feet back, try to get up. You can't do it!

When you sit up straight, you're supported by the seat of the chair. The vertical line through your center of gravity falls within your base and you're "at rest." You can't get up until you've changed your center of gravity so that the vertical line

248

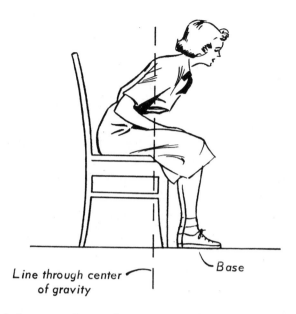

Line through center
of gravity

Base

through it goes through your new base . . . your feet.
To do this you either have to lean forward to bring
your center of gravity above your feet or you have
to pull your feet back under your chair to bring
your new base under your center of gravity. Most
of the time you do a little of both without giving
what you're doing a bit of thought.

Here's a trick you can try on a friend. When
you see how he reacts, have him try it on you. You'll
react in the same way, even when you know what
the trick's all about.

EXPERIMENT 136

Materials: Two pencils

A friend

Gently press the points of two pencils held together against the back of your friend's neck.

Ask him to tell you how many pencils are touching his neck. He'll answer, "One!" Try just one pencil and he'll still say one. Don't laugh at him. You won't be able to tell the difference when he tries it on you. Before you do that, however, have your friend close his eyes and then you touch one and two pencils to the tips of his fingers.

He'll call out the number of pencils touching his fingers without any trouble at all.

While it's true you can feel things touch you all over your body, some areas of your body are more sensitive to touch than others because the endings of the nerves that react to touch are closer together in some parts than in others. You use your fingers to touch things all day long and so they're very sensitive. You can readily tell whether there are one or two pencils on your fingers. But the touch-sensitive nerve endings are so far apart on the back of your neck, you can't tell the difference between one or two pencil points. The tip of your tongue is even more sensitive than the tips of your fingers.

Let's examine some of your other senses. Let's take seeing first, and find out what good two eyes are.

EXPERIMENT 137

Materials: Your hands

With your hands at your sides, point both forefingers (those you point with) at the ground and double up the rest of your fingers. Now close one eye and raise both arms out in front of you. Try to bring the tips of your forefingers together so they touch.

It's hard to do! Before you try it again, drop your arms down to your sides. You can do it with little trouble when you use both of your eyes. Why is it so hard with one eye? It's hard because you need two eyes to judge distances away from you accurately. Each eye sees the thing you're looking at from a slightly different angle because your eyes are set apart. Your brain combines these two slightly different images into one. But the difference in the two views is what tells you how far away the object is from you. The range finder of a camera works on the same principle. When you use only one eye your brain receives only one view and distances are hard for you to judge.

If you've never noticed the fact that each of your eyes sees a slightly different view, try this.

EXPERIMENT 138

Materials: Your thumb

Hold one hand straight out in front of you with your thumb pointing straight up. Close your right eye and with your left, line up your thumb with something across the room like one side of a door.

Now close your left eye and open your right. Your thumb is now lined up with the other side of the door!

Each eye sees a different view of the door and when you line up your thumb and the door with your left eye, they're out of line with your right eye.

What good are two ears?

EXPERIMENT 139

Materials: One ear

Two spoons

A friend

Stand behind your friend and have him put a finger in one of his ears to shut off sounds. Tell him

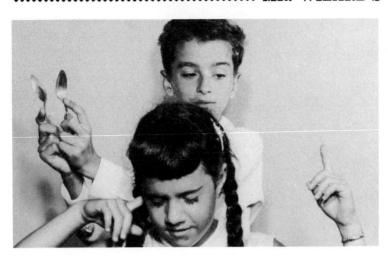

you're going to click two spoons together. He's supposed to point in the direction the sound comes from. Betsy certainly was confused when Willy tried this stunt on her.

Betsy, your friend and you, when you try it, will have trouble telling where the sound comes from because you need two ears to do it most of the time. Like each of your eyes sees a different view, each of your ears hears a slight difference in the volume of sound, especially when the sound comes from one side. The ear closest to the sound hears it a little louder than the ear that's farther away. Your brain automatically tells you which ear is hearing the louder sound, and that's how you know which side the sound is coming from. With one ear closed and the sound coming from various positions on that side, your brain has only one message coming to it, and you can't tell where the sound is coming from with any accuracy.

Do you like roast beef? Most people do because they like the taste of it. But you don't taste roast beef . . . you smell it!

EXPERIMENT 140

Materials: Piece of roast beef

Before you get the roast beef anywhere near your mouth, hold your nose so you can't smell. Then put the roast beef in your mouth.

The roast beef will be a tasteless piece of meat in your mouth. Now take your fingers away from your nose and inhale. Suddenly you can "taste" the roast beef! Your sense of taste and smell work together so closely that you can't tell them apart much of the time. Sometimes the "taste" of food in your mouth comes from your sense of smell in your nose, sometimes from your sense of taste in your tongue, and sometimes from both at the same time. Roast beef "tastes" like roast beef only when you can smell it. Sugar, on the other hand, you can't smell at all. You can't even taste it when it's dry.

EXPERIMENT 141

Materials: Teaspoon of sugar

Clean towel

This is one time you can stick out your tongue in the interest of science because you want to wipe it dry with a *clean* towel. Keeping your tongue out and dry, sprinkle some sugar on it from the teaspoon.

There the sweet sugar sits right on your tongue and you can't taste it! For you to taste any food, it must be dissolved in water. When you put dry food into your mouth it has to be dissolved in the saliva before you can taste it. No wonder your mouth "waters" when you're hungry. Put your tongue back in your mouth and moisten it with saliva. Now you can taste the sugar. As you swallow the sugar in your mouth, you're opening a trap door.

EXPERIMENT 142

Materials: A swallow

Touch one hand to your throat with the thumb on one side and the fingers on the other side of your "Adam's apple."

Now swallow. Feel your "Adam's apple" go up and then down? There are two passages going down from your mouth. One is for air and the other is for food. When you're breathing, the food passage is closed by a "trap door" so the air will go down the other passage. When you swallow food, the motion you feel is partly the trap door swinging away from the food passage to open it and at the same time close off the air passage. The food then goes down the right "tunnel." When "something goes down the wrong throat," or you get something caught in the trap door, an emergency signal is sent to a remote-control message center inside of you (your brain), and things happen fast. Your coughing is your body's way of trying to dislodge whatever is stuck in the trap door. This doesn't happen very often. Most of the time the trap door opens, the food goes through and the trap door closes. What happens to the food going down the "tunnel" to your stomach? Does it just fall down there with a "plunk" like a rock falling into a well? No, it doesn't.

EXPERIMENT 143

Materials: An apple

A pillow or cushion

Lay the pillow on the floor near the wall. Stand on your head on the pillow and brace your feet against the wall. Now eat the apple. I mean it! When you've taken a bite, chew it well and then

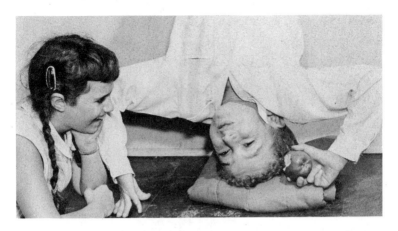

swallow it. It goes right *up* to your stomach. Betsy laughed at how funny Willy looked eating an apple upside down. Willy said Betsy looked just as funny to him.

You can swallow things upside down because your food passage has muscles that tighten behind the food pushing it along to your stomach. What happens to the food when it reaches your stomach and intestines is a very complicated chemical process which you call "digesting."

When you've eaten and digested the proper food, your body has to distribute it to all of its parts. This is done by your blood. The blood is kept circulating in your body by your heart. Let's examine your heart.

Place the fingers of one hand on the wrist of your other hand.

You may have to move your fingers around a little to feel the blood surging through the blood vessel that lies near the surface of your wrist. That's what the doctor's doing when he "takes your pulse." He counts the number of surges in a half a minute or a minute to find out how fast your heart is beating.

255

Your pulse "beats" in rhythm with your heart. Magnify your pulse like this so that you can actually see it beat.

EXPERIMENT 144

Materials: Match

Thumbtack

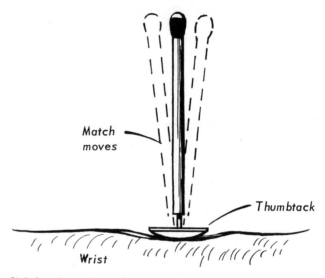

Match moves

Thumbtack

Wrist

Stick the thumbtack into the bottom of the match. Place the thumbtack over your pulse. When you get it just right the match will move back and forth with every beat of your heart.

You've seen the matchstick move with the pulsing of your blood. Here's how you can hear your own heart beat.

EXPERIMENT 145

Materials: Small funnel

Rubber tubing

Push the small end of the funnel into the rubber

tubing and hold the other end of the tubing to your ear. Hold the large end of the funnel to your chest. Move your home-made stethoscope around until you can hear the beating of your heart.

You'll find your heart is nearer the middle of your chest than you thought. The sound you hear is caused by the vibrations sent through your body when the valves of your heart open and close and blood is pumped in and out of the various parts.

When you watched bubbles at work, I said you breathed out carbon dioxide that was the result of the "slow burning" or oxidizing of food in your body. You breathe in air to get the oxygen that's necessary. Your blood carries the oxygen to all parts of your body as well as carrying away the carbon dioxide. The O_2 goes into the blood and the CO_2 comes out of it in your lungs. Here's how your lungs work.

EXPERIMENT 146

Materials: **Lamp chimney**

Glass tube with a "Y" at one end

Rubber stopper

Small balloons

Large balloon

Rubber bands

Put the materials together as they are in the drawing. Cut the large balloon in half and stretch it over the bottom of the lamp chimney. Hold it securely in place with rubber bands. Note the parts of your body that correspond with the things in the lamp chimney. The air in the lamp chimney itself is trapped there by the stopper on the top and the rubber balloon on the bottom. The outside air can go in

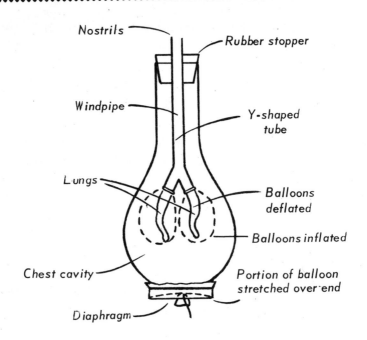

and out of the small balloons by means of the Y-shaped tube. When you push the large balloon up, you put pressure on the air inside the lamp chimney. This forces the air in the small balloons out of the tube. This is similar to what happens when you exhale or breathe out. When you pull the large balloon down you make the air inside the lamp chimney expand. This lowers the pressure inside the chimney and the outside air (under atmospheric pressure) flows down the tube and expands the small balloons. This is similar to what happens when you inhale or breathe in.

The oxygen and the food in your blood are carried to all parts of your body. Each part has a special job to do, but all of them need the oxygen and the food in it. In your muscles, for example, the oxygen and the food are used to build tissue and make the muscle move. Bend your arm. As your muscles move they're taking in oxygen and food and giving out carbon dioxide and waste materials.

Bend your arm again. Did you know that your muscles can move in only one direction? It's true. Your muscles are body tissues that can only contract or tighten up. They can't expand or loosen by themselves. You'll understand this better when you make a model of your arm out of wood.

EXPERIMENT 147

Materials: **Wood**

Rubber bands

String

Screw eyes

Washer

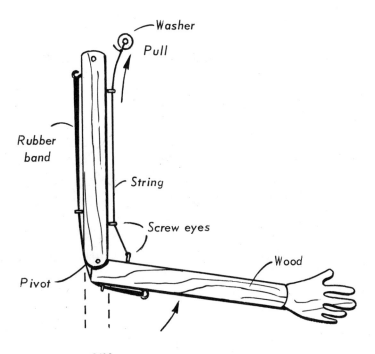

259

You can see from the model of your arm that the string that represents the muscle on the front of your upper arm pulls your forearm up. This stretches the rubber band that represents the muscle on the back of your upper arm. When you relax the front or bending muscle and tighten the back muscle your arm unbends. You coordinate your muscle movements without thinking by relaxing one when you tighten the other. But each muscle can only move in one direction as it tightens or gets smaller.

Hold your hand out in front of you. The muscles you're using must continue to stay tight or "under tension" to keep your hand steady. This muscle tension makes your hand move so slightly it's hardly noticeable. This almost unnoticeable muscle movement is the science secret behind a walking hairpin.

EXPERIMENT 148

Materials: Table knife

Hairpin

Hold the knife in one hand parallel to the top of the table. Do not touch the table with your hand or arm. Slip the hairpin around the knife. Raise the knife just high enough for the "feet" of the hairpin to touch the table and the "head" of the hairpin to rest on the knife edge. Hold the knife as steady as you can. Try as you will to stop it, the hairpin walks right down the knife edge!

The small movements of the muscles in your arm move the knife edge up and down slightly. When the edge is up the hairpin's feet are pulled along the table. When the edge is down the feet keep the hairpin from backing up and the head moves further down

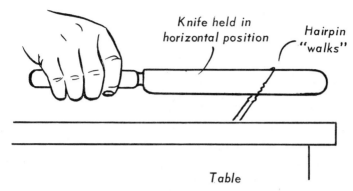

Knife held in horizontal position

Hairpin "walks"

Table

the knife. The next up-movement of the edge holds the head firm and the feet walk a couple of steps. The tighter you hold your hand and arm to stop the hairpin from walking, the more tension there is in your muscles and the faster it walks!

Your muscle tension and movement become greater as your muscles get tired. Scientists use this fact for testing how tired your muscles are. Here's a tension tester that will give you more fun than facts about your muscles.

EXPERIMENT 149

Materials: **Wood**

Copper wire

Flashlight bulb in base

Door bell

Battery

Wire

Nails

Screws

Hook up your tension tester so that when the nail touches the copper wire it acts like a switch and the bulb lights and the door bell rings. You may

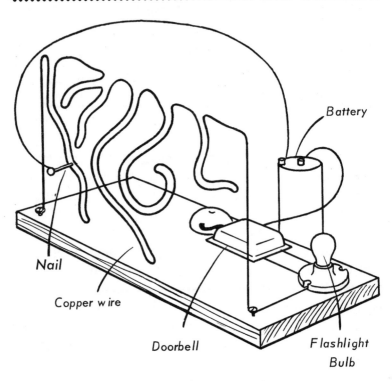

Battery

Nail

Copper wire

Doorbell

Flashlight
Bulb

need more than one dry cell to make both the light
and the door bell work well. The object of the tension
tester is to see how many times you touch the copper
wire as you run the nail down into the long loops of
wire and back out again. The person who lights the
light and rings the bell the least number of times
has the steadiest hand and the best control of his
muscles. You can make the tension tester more difficult to do by pulling the wires of the loops closer
together and making the curves tighter.

Scientists have studied how your body works for
a long time and they're still studying it. They've
solved a lot of the mysteries, but there are still more
to be solved. That's why I said the biggest mystery
of all was you. But now that you've seen how some

of the parts of your body work, perhaps you'll realize better than you did before what an amazing and wonderful thing it is. And you can see why it's so important to take good care of it by following the rules of good health: get plenty of rest, sleep, exercise and water and eat three well-balanced meals a day.

Well, you've been investigating the mysteries of the magic of science in the world around you. I hope my science secrets have helped you solve some of the mysteries and perform some of the magic. Do you remember the first experiment? I asked you to look at a mystery that was right in front of your nose. Turn the page, look right in front of your nose again and you'll see another mystery. To solve it, close one eye, hold the book level to your eye and look flat across the page.

TURN PAGE FOR THE LAST EXPERIMENT!

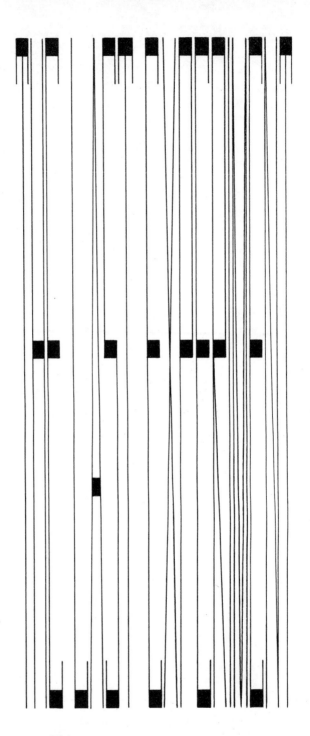